BUILDING WARRIORS

West Point Judo's
Road to the National Championship

TRANSFORMATIONAL COACHING IN ACTION

HECTOR MORALES NEGRON, Ph.D., CC-AASP

Lieutenant Colonel, USA (Retired)

PMG
PEAK MENTAL GAME
OPTIMAL PERFORMANCE EDUCATION

BUILDING WARRIORS

West Point Judo's Road to the National Championship

TRANSFORMATIONAL COACHING IN ACTION

Published by Peak Mental Game: Optimal Performance
Education, LLC

Printed and distributed by Createspace

514 River Crane St

Bradenton, FL 34212

Hector Morales-Negrón

peakmentalgame@gmail.com

850-459-1498

Paperback ISBN-10: 0-9983547-0-8

ISBN-13: 978-0-9983547-0-5

Printed in the United States of America

First Edition 2016

Front Cover Photo: Courtesy of Academy Photo; U.S.
Military Academy Flickr (2011)

Back Cover Photo: Courtesy of Michael Shattan (2010)

Table of Contents

Foreword by Mr. Bud Burrell, West Point Judo Class 1968, First West Point Judo NCJA Medalist

I wanted to write a letter of commendation for this book on the U. S. Military Academy Judo Program you re-started with your assignment as an Academy Professor in 2008.

What you did with your students over just a five-year period borders on the miraculous. Few can appreciate the complexity of either Sports Judo or Combatives. I gave over 30 years of my life to studying Judo and other Combatives Arts such as Small Circle Ju-jitsu, various forms of Karate including Wing Chung, Shotokan, Goju, Escrima, and much more. Around these myriad studies, I managed to stuff in 14 years of hard competition with some noted successes, constantly disrupted by duty demands.

I can say that although I had some great coaches, I only worked with two teams of significance: the USMA Judo Team of 1967-1968 with Coach Tom Cress from the New York Athletic Club and the Black Belt School of Judo in Atlanta from 1974 to 1976, with Coaches Bruce Toups and George Flanagan.

My career progress significantly interfered with my Judo, kind of a price of poker, particularly difficult with the Army, but even more so in my jobs on Wall Street. Conversely, being sent to many places around this country, I had to study what was available, when I could.

Judo was a "Spring Club" sport when I was a Cadet, meaning our full out practice was only three months a year, actually less. We were always playing start-up each year with each seasonal break.

With the program you instituted of five days a week, year-round practice with frequent contests, you broke through the barriers to accelerated learning, and improved player and coaching development. More importantly, you created a bonding of your students and coaches that was inspirational. You were the first coach at the Academy I ever heard of who could integrate Male and Female students in a hard contact sport with no friction.

You achieved absolute success from year one of your tenure as Officer-in-Charge and Coach of the Judo Club. When you won the National Collegiate Judo Association Team Title beginning in 2010, mouths fell open. I was remotely jacked by your success, as were the many who knew you from your prior work.

The NCJA was founded in 1962 by the legendary coach Yosh Uchida of San Jose State, which won more than 40 National Collegiate Judo Team Titles in just 50 years. Your efforts resulted in the USMA team displacing their reign.

A West Point Graduate from the Class of 1948, Phil Porter, who came out of work with the Air Force Judo Team that dominated US Judo in the 1960's, had founded the Armed Forces Judo Association and USJA, was Uchida Sensei's cofounder of the NCJA. Porter Sensei went on to Coach the NJI (the National Judo Institute in Colorado Springs for 15 years), which he used to produce over 1000 Judo winners both domestically and internationally.

Over the years, some coaches who preceded you had experiences that laid out a roadmap for someone who followed on how to build a real "Team." Great instructors such as Tom Cress, an Olympic Team Alternate in 1972, and MSG Ramon Ancho, a legend in Special Forces and a ranked Master in Judo and many other arts.

What you did was to coalesce the many lessons you and these men had learned into one place and one time, adding your very valuable input as a competitor and coach, with astonishing results.

The story told here could be a road map of how to build an incredible team in any activity, but most certainly in start-ups of any kind.

Because of your efforts and your Team's results, you and Professor Reno would receive the noted "Coach K" awards for the outstanding achievements as Coaches at USMA.

People talk a great deal about what student-athletes in other Colleges and Universities must handle, but what a student at USMA face is incredible. Your athletes not only managed those challenges, but they also had to learn and apply a complicated event like Judo as a national level competitive sport.

You encountered many barriers in your work, ones that I hope your book will be used for in the future Student Activities for other successful efforts.

Again, you embody the very traits you embedded in your Cadets. They have been given a gift to have encountered you and to have experienced what your kind of demands could give them in the future.

NO LIMITS.

Very Best Regards,

C. Austin (Bud) Burrell, Class of 1968, CIC of Judo Club, 1967-1968

Eastern Collegiate Champion 1967, 1st Place, 165 lbs. at ECJA Championships held at West Point, Runner-Up for Grand Championship

3rd place, 165 lbs. NCJA Championships, held at San Jose State

Dedication

This book is dedicated to my wife, Marisol, and my kids: Meagan, Hector, and Francisco. They all embraced the military and Judo journeys and made it part of their experience. They connected with the athletes and took them in as extended members of our family. West Point Judo became a family affair, and they have been there through the ups and the downs. They also know that even when I love Judo, they ARE the MOST important part of my life.

To Mom, because she gave it all for us. Carried the weight on her shoulders and motivated us always to follow our dreams.

To Dr. Richard Hagen, a mentor and driving force for turning a young non-English speaking kid into a leader of men who could reach unexpected feats.

A special dedication to all West Point Judokas. Over 50 years of fighters and warriors

who went on to fight our nation's wars. Godspeed
to all of you!

Acknowledgments

There are many stories to share about my nine years as the coach of the West Point Judo team. The majority of these stories are positive and one of my biggest rewards while working with the cadet-athletes was when I got the chance to see them again, as officers, and they became involved with the program. Three of those officers are an integral part of this story. Without their hard work and support, the team's achievements described in this book would not have been possible. Working at West Point keeps you busy and finding time to give to something you are passionate about requires a huge sacrifice in personal and family time. In addition, the academy has an incredible group of men and women who support cadets in all their endeavors. For those of you on this list please know that you have a special spot in my heart and that I cherish our relationships.

LTC Mike Shattan, West Point Class 1999. A member of the early team/program who became the Officer in Charge (OIC) in 2011 and conducted all supporting and logistical tasks for the team's daily operations and travel.

MAJ Jonathan D. Baker, West Point Class 2001. He was a member of the 2001 runner-up National Team. He took over as the OIC during the 2012 season.

MAJ Travis Tilman, West Point Class 2000. He came back to the team in the role of mental skills coach for the 2010 and 2011 seasons.

Reno Claudio, Assistant Coach for all my nine seasons at West Point. He was a father figure to me as well as my right hand in all Judo operations. Also, he was responsible for the novice technical development program.

Daniel Lorenzen, A lifelong learner that committed to the program. Dan took over as OIC during the 2013 and 2014 season and kept the program running after my departure in 2014.

Tony Notaro, Volunteer Assistant to Mr. Claudio. While not a Judo man, Tony helped Reno with the novice athletes and was always present to support the mission.

BG (R) Greg Daniels, Master of the Sword, Director, Department of Physical Education and **COL (R) Jesse Germain**, Deputy Director. Without their support, my time and opportunities to guide the Judo Team would not have existed. They understood the contributions of these programs to cadet development and supported our involvement.

Dr. Ralph Pim, Director of Competitive Sports, Department of Physical Education. Our vision and passion for developing leaders through sports were aligned. His program provided a great atmosphere for teams to thrive and reach their maximum potential.

Mr. Bud Burrell, 1st West Point Judo Athlete to Place at the NCJA. Mr. Burrell followed the team and tracked our performance. I credit him for the encouragement to write this book.

DCA Supporting Staff, the women in the DCA staff: **Carol, Renee, Maria, Donna,** and all the great people that worked extremely hard behind the scenes to support the cadets' activities.

Department of Physical Education Supporting Staff, led by Mr. Artie Coughlin and Vince Stock who supported every training event and tournament held at Arvin Cadet Physical Development Center.

West Point Judo Alumni. Thanks for taking the time to share your stories and perspectives. The West Point Judo experience through your eyes is the core foundation of this book.

Ladies and gentlemen, you are all part of this West Point Judo journey, and you contributed greatly to this story.

Baker, Tilman, Shattan, Morales, Reno, and Tony
at the 2011 Championships

About this Book

I wrote this book with two primary motives in mind. First, I want to share the West Point Judo story. The athletes on this team mean the world to me and they worked extremely hard to accomplish something no one expected them to achieve. I believe their story needs to be told, they also must understand the back-story so they continue to feel proud of their development and their accomplishments as cadet-athletes. The relationships that we built are special, and I hope that the experience influenced their lives as much as it impacted mine. Secondly, this book is about leadership and transformational coaching. It is designed to help you see the application of some basic leadership concepts through the lens of the West Point Judo program. I am a firm believer that these tenets and stories can also be applied to other competitive and professional settings. If you want to develop a winning culture that builds character, this book can provide you with an excellent start.

The U.S. Military Academy is recognized as one of the most prominent leader development institutions in the world. The Judo mat was one additional laboratory for the development of future U.S. Army leaders. On that mat, these cadet-athletes learned to set goals and develop a plan to achieve them. They learned to trust their training and their teammates under the most physically demanding conditions any competitive setting can offer. They learned to manage their ego daily after every win and after every loss. They learned what it feels like to have an opponent breathing in their faces, trying to subdue and defeat them. They learned that hard work could beat talent and that if they trusted their training, they could be feared, and they could defeat anyone. They learned to train their minds at the same level they trained their bodies and to control their emotions regardless of the situation. They saw that leaders could show that they are human and vulnerable without losing the respect of the people they lead. They learned that a true team takes care of each other on and off the mat. Lastly, they set the standard for gender relationships at the Military Academy as these warriors trained, fought, and won together.

The strategies in this book are proven to build warriors, teams of significance, and a winning culture. They were the building blocks of West Point Judo's success and legacy from 2009 until 2014. These strategies now become available for you to use in programs, businesses, and at the personal level to create more opportunities and paths to higher levels of performance.

Hope you enjoy the ride as much as we did.

Yours in Development,

DrM

Chapter 1 – Passion is Your Foundation

"Passion will move men beyond themselves, beyond their shortcomings, beyond their failures."

Joseph Campbell

Puerto Rico hosted the 1979 Pan American Games, and a couple of months before the games, I had the privilege to carry the Pan Am flame torch for about a mile in my town and was part of the opening ceremonies activities. Because my father was responsible for the sports program in our town, I followed every sport and was at every event I could participate. As I ran the mile, I felt connected with the passion I was developing for sport, performance, and physical education.

I can clearly remember that throughout my life, I have always started reading the newspapers backward. In the front pages, you normally find a daily dose of human failures and tragedies that steal from your soul and take away from your enjoyment and preparation for the day. In the sports pages, you find stories of success and elements of peak human performance that give us hope and inspiration. It is easy to become passionate about sports and physical activity because we also get to enjoy some immediate feedback on our progress. At the beginning of a training session, we may not know a technique, but with effort and repetition, we may walk away with the satisfaction of executing the task. In sports settings, the passion you develop along the way is truly needed. In these competitive settings, you will also be challenged, physically and mentally, people will try to diminish what you are passionate about, and you will be tested with adversity. I say, stay the course. Your passion will take you far, as it is the primary ingredient to becoming gritty, and grit will allow you to enjoy what you do and will allow you to stick with it. Lock that passion in, use it as a shield against that adversity until you can embrace it and make it your own. In this book, there are multiple examples of how passion can keep you going.

Without it, there would be no West Point Judo story.

At age 13, I started doing martial arts training with a group of friends and chose to stick with Judo and wrestling out of all the arts that we had exposure to. I loved the opportunity that these sports provided to earn your spot. Making the team was not a personality contest, and it was not solely in the hands of the coach. You had to fight for your spot, and there was no doubt if the spot was yours or if you got beat and had to prepare better to try the next time again. In my eyes, this is as fair as anything can be. The sport became part of my passion, and I decided right then that it would be part of my professional path. When we were at West Point, my wife used to ask me, "You can do so many things at a time, how can you do that?"

My response was simple. "When you met me, I was a Judo athlete, a ROTC cadet, and a physical education student. About 20 years later, I am Judo coach, an Army officer, and an academy professor of physical education. Not much has changed, I was just passionate about all these three areas of my life and was never willing to let any of them go." My passion allowed me to be persistent to the point that I had no choice but to reach success regardless of the trials along the way.

Challenges will be part of our development. At times, we will be close to our goal but will stumble. At times, we will have developed a great rhythm and are on pace to get what we want and BAM!, life throws changes at you. At times, your fire may seem to go away, but when you look hard enough, you may find that a little flame remains and you can re-ignite what you believe in and what you were working to accomplish. Your passion will help you stay the course, your passion will help you overcome challenges, and your passion will lead you to impact others and succeed in ways that you never imagined. Connect with it now, never give up on what you want;

learn to adapt, but always keep your goals and passion in mind.

Chapter 2 - Judo: A Way of Life

"When I first stepped into the dojo and tried out for the team, I knew that it was where I wanted to be. The energy from LTC Morales and Sensei Reno and the other team members was simply incredible. Experienced teachers were eager to coach, and members of the team were equally eager to train. The team genuinely cared for one another — always wearing a smile, willing to help, and committed to learning the art of Judo. I think back and cannot help but feel an intense sense of gratitude and happiness. I found a family away from home and friendships that will last a lifetime. Judo truly changed my life — physically, mentally, and spiritually. Judo has and will always be more than a sport to me. It is a lifestyle and a community that I am so proud to be a part of."

Ariel Espinosa-Levy, West Point Class 2012

NCJA Medalist and 2012 Brigade Grappling Champion

The drive from Judo practice to the medical "expert" lady in my neighborhood appeared to be a quiet one, but inside my head, there was a storm brewing. I could not move my left arm; my shoulder was locked up. Thoughts of guilt sparked my anger and clouded my thinking. My internal overpowering negative voice destroyed me on what felt like a six-hour drive. While it was only 45 minutes, the intense pain and the internal dialogue got the best of me.

"You should have listened."

"You did not need that additional practice."

"You have thrown it all away."

As an eager developmental collegiate Judo athlete, I was on my third practice of the day. I was not supposed to be there, my Sensei (coach) advised me against it, but the mind of that young man was made up. Because I loved my sport and I wanted to improve, I assumed that more was going to be better.

"One more fight, Hector?" said Jose after I had already removed my Gi (Judo uniform)

"No, I am done for today, thanks. We will catch up tomorrow." I should have left; that should have been my final statement. However, what-ifs and

should-haves are like Monday morning quarterbacking, useless.

"*Come on man, are you afraid?*" said Jose sarcastically. And it was on!

Pride will blind you; pride will make you do and say things you do not need to do nor say. I went in. "*One more fight, what is the worst that can happen?*" I said to myself. After several minutes battling, back and forth, I came in for a clear throw. I was confident. Jose stepped back and countered my technique. I was in the air and falling fast. For a split second, pride got the best of me once again. "*Don't let him put you on your back, throw your arm out and stop the fall,*" I thought. The third bad decision of the day and this one landed me in this lady's living room. She was not a doctor, a nurse, or medical practitioner, but she was the one everyone in my neighborhood went to for medical advice.

She asked me, "*Can you lift your arm?*"

"*No, I can't.*"

She felt my shoulder and said,"*It is out of the socket. We need to put it back.*" I thought about what my sensei told me earlier. I thought about my opportunities to continue to compete, so I looked at her and nodded my head in agreement. She asked me to bite my belt. She grabbed my arm by the elbow and placed her foot on the chair. "*Hold on!*" she said shortly before pulling sharply. Suddenly, I heard a pop and felt an intense pain. I had never felt anything like it before and yet; my only thought was *when can I get back on the mat again?* I know now that this is what it feels like when something becomes part of you. Judo was not only my sport, but it was also my lifestyle; it had become my way of life.

The tenants of Judo which include maximum efficiency and mutual welfare and benefit are preached at practice and are expected to be integrated as part of the participant's approach to life. I learned these concepts and tried to apply them to all areas of my professional and personal life doubling down on making Judo part of who I was.

Judo is an addictive sport. Judo is a blue-collar type sport. Judo is a way of life and is a sport that gets very little recognition in the United States even when it is the second most practiced sport throughout the world. Outside of everyone recognizing the notorious Hollywood's "Judo Chop" (which, by the way, does not happen in the sports application of Judo) and those who follow mixed martial arts closely, with the recent exposure of some exceptional athletes in the Ultimate Fighting Championships (UFC), many people don't know the specifics of this great art. At the 2016 Olympics, two exceptional U.S. Judo athletes: Kayla Harrison and Travis Stevens took gold and silver respectively which is the best performance ever at the Olympics for USA Judo. Even then, I found myself explaining what Judo is about to too many people. People who do Judo are passionate and probably fell in love with the sport the same way that I did, from their first exposure.

Judo is a martial art developed in 1882 by a professor and scholar, Dr. Jigoro Kano, with the purpose of educating young minds and bodies through exposure to self-defense and proper training. It is a Japanese Martial Art and a sport practiced worldwide that surpassed the expectations of its creator regarding numbers of participants. He wanted to use this art as a system for developing young people, a system of physical education with a discipline component. Little did he know that almost a hundred years later, his vision would provide opportunities for a young man from Puerto Rico to be educated, developed, and exposed to great experiences that allowed him to see the world. That young man learned to love the sport and impacted the development of thousands of others students utilizing similar methods of training.

In the United States, the sport began to spread during the 1950s as American service members brought their training experiences back from Japan. These early leaders started schools and organizations that were the roots of the current national organizations responsible for the development of Judo in the U.S. In Judo, athletes begin their matches facing each other in the center of the mat. The primary objective is to obtain a dominant grip on their opponent and break their balance with the intent of throwing them to the ground. If your opponent lands fully on their back, the match is over. If an effective throw is executed quickly, the match can be over in as little as two seconds. On the other hand, it can last up to five minutes with a deciding throw executed at minute four with 59 seconds. There is no safe lead in the sport of Judo; you must fight the entire match. If the throw is not perfect, the fight will continue on the ground where victories can be scored with control holds by pinning your opponent to the ground for 20 seconds, strangulation techniques, and joint locking techniques. A sport requires athletes to have and constantly demonstrate warrior ethos, stamina, and perseverance among other key qualities. For those who watch Judo for the first time, it looks more like Olympic wrestling than any of the other martial arts because there are not kicks or strikes in competitive Judo matches. The similarities in wrestling and Judo extend to the physical requirements and the grappling element on the ground. During my college days, we were expected to compete in both sports during our athletic experience.

West Point Judo Origins: The Inspiration of the Old Class

The West Point Judo program was built on persistence and is an incredible story of passion and perseverance that was first shared with me by COL (R) Dave McLaughlin when I met him at the U.S. Judo Senior Nationals in Houston, Texas in 2000. He and his family traveled to Houston from San Antonio to support cadets participating at the national event. During our first engagement, he told me the story of the 1962 team, the first West Point Judo Team. McLaughlin's roommate, Cadet Lee Taylor, was a Judo black belt, and he asked him to teach him the sport. The group started very small with some volunteers trying to get acceptance to become an official club. The leadership of the academy at the time had served in World War II and therefore originally resisted the approval a Japanese-based art and sport within the walls of the Academy. The cadets were denied several times but continued to use their personal time for training and competition, eventually reaching a good level of success.

In 1962 Yosh Uchida of San Jose State University and Phil Porter, a West Point graduate working at the Air Force Academy, also established the National Collegiate Judo Association. West Point has been part of this organization from its beginning. Over the years, cadets attended the NCJA tournament with limited success. However, at the regional level, cadets thrived mostly because of their physicality, stamina, and will to win.

The West Point Judo Men's Team has been in existence for over four decades before its members earned the right to call themselves national champions. Based on the NCJA historical records, the 1994 women's team won a title with three competitive athletes but was unable to repeat the feat for almost two decades. The development of a new culture would bring them together under a mission that would change the way everyone looked at them as Judokas and as warriors. However, the transition was not easy. As a competitive club at the U.S. Military Academy with limited support, low priority, and volunteer coaches, as well as competing against programs nationwide with more advanced and experienced Judokas, it was an uphill battle.

Back Row: Taylor (Coach), Patterson, McCoy, Werner, Yamashita (Coach)
Middle Row: Spencer, Bitters, McLaughlin, Dueñas
Front Row: Jenison, Nelson, Bernard, Watters

First West Point Judo Team circa 1962

New Black Belts for Cadets of Class 2012 with

Col (R) McLaughlin, member of the first Army Judo Team

(Photo Courtesy of BySoledad Photography)

Chapter 3 - Every Cadet an Athlete – Welcome to the Department of Physical Education

"On the fields of friendly strife are sown the seeds that on other days, on other fields, will bear the fruits of victory."

General Douglas MacArthur

The graduation ceremony for the Class of 2014 of the U.S. Military Academy was about to begin. This time, unlike the previous eight years as a faculty member and Academy professor, when I was on the field, I sat in the stands as a newly retired officer. I could see the back of the gray uniforms of the thousand cadets of the class of 2014 that were about to begin their military journey. The sun was shining and yet the center stage was full of stars as several general officers marched on marking the actual beginning of the ceremony. As the generals and the President of the United States marched on stage, my mind floated to a much earlier phase of my career. In my mind, I was back in 1998 when I first reported to the

Academy as a rotating instructor in the Department of Physical Education. It was there when the dream to build a championship team at West Point was born. However, the motivation to teach and coach that brought me to the Academy started much earlier in my life.

As a child, I became fascinated with the physical education field. I played traditional sports but out of the necessity to improve fitness and for self-defense started training in martial arts at the age of 13. In the beginning, I trained with a group of friends by reading martial arts books, conducting physical training, and applying the techniques to self-defense scenarios. Out of all the arts that I had exposure to, I focused my training in wrestling and Judo. I had no idea how many doors that exposure would open and the future that laid ahead because of my relationship with the sport of Judo. At an early age, I identified that I was passionate about teaching and coaching, so I attended the University of Puerto Rico to study physical education. While at the University, I competed in wrestling and Judo for four years under the guidance of Sensei Hiromi Tomita. As a collegiate athlete, I had the privilege to contribute to several championship teams in both Judo and wrestling by earning gold medals. Upon graduating from the UPR, I received a Bachelor's Degree in physical education and a commission in the U.S. Army as a second lieutenant.

My physical education degree was very useful as an Army officer as I focused many of my efforts in the physical and mental development of my soldiers and to prepare them to compete in everything they did. After serving as a platoon leader, I returned to Judo competition and continued my development in physical education. In 1993, I met Dr. Sue Tendy while attending the U.S. Army Master Fitness Trainer Course. Dr. Tendy told me about the Department of Physical Education (DPE) at the U.S. Military Academy. She told me the department was responsible for the physical development of all the cadets and future leaders. She also mentioned that in the department, faculty instructed combatives, Judo, and Boxing and that I would fit in as a faculty member. That conversation changed my career as I began the process to be selected and work in this great environment as DPE had a very competitive process to fill their limited rotating faculty spots. As an officer, physical educator, and athlete, I would be where all my passions collided.

I started to learn more about the Department of Physical Education (DPE) and found out about their policy that requires every cadet to participate in a sport or competitive event. This approach had its foundation on General MacArthur's quote at the beginning of this chapter. "Every cadet an athlete" was a concept that appealed to me, as it was part of my personal foundation as a leader. My efforts, training, and lessons on the mat clearly influenced my leadership approach, the success of my units, and the development of my Soldiers. It made sense to me that, through sports, we could provide the opportunity for individuals to grow and demonstrate their character. Ultimately, I wanted to contribute to this program and be part of this department more than anything.

I was a young captain in Germany in 1997 when I was selected to teach in DPE and arrived at the Academy in the summer of 1998 after completing my Master's in kinesiology at the University of Georgia. The department was what I expected it to be; it was full of professionals and experts in their respective fields of aquatics, gymnastics, combatives, and fitness and wellness. Also, there were sport-specific courses and many other opportunities for cadets to grow in their physical development.

At West Point, cadets are required to participate in one of three options for their athletic experience. They can participate as part of the Corps' Squad program which includes all the sports that participate in NCAA Division I competition. The second option is for cadets to participate in what was initially called intramural sports. This program would later, under the leadership of Dr. Ralph Pim, be renamed company level athletics. In this option, cadets participate as members of a company (unit) team that competes in one of the five or six sports provided per academic term. The last opportunity available is for cadets to be part of a team under the competitive clubs' program. The competitive club program allowed faculty members to volunteer to coach and teach sports that were not offered as part of the Corps' Squad-NCAA sports. These clubs could still represent and compete against other universities. Back in 1998, there were about 19 competitive clubs that included boxing, Judo, fencing, rugby, rowing among others. The best part of these competitive clubs was the concept that the cadets got the opportunity to choose which activity they wanted to develop as student-athletes. They trained for two hours a day, and these were probably the only two hours in their cadet day where they had the chance to do something they chose to do.

It was in this program that I was first given the opportunity to become a coach. While I had led teams before, it was never as a head coach. I arrived at the Academy fresh out of my last international competition where I represented the US at the First World Military Games in Rome. After that event, I was a member of a team in Germany and then put my Judo Gi away during my command, during deployments in support of IFOR and SFOR in Bosnia, and most of my Master's Degree education. Before arriving at West Point, I read Brigadier General (R) James Anderson book on training the Weekend Competitive Athlete where he described the programs sponsored by the department. He introduced the Judo team and its beginnings.

When I arrived at DPE, I met the coach of the program. He had a different training approach than mine, and in the beginning, it appeared impossible for me to be able to coach with him. Our coaching philosophies, training approaches, and passion for the sport of Judo were at two different levels. Luckily, that coach saw me as an opportunity to take a break and conduct some research. The door was open; I was going to be able to contribute to the development of warriors, fighters that one day would use their experiences on the mat to be better leaders. I believed that using that time to grow athletes' character, physical stamina, skill to fight, and their ability to close with the enemy was a unique opportunity to impact leader development.

Knowing that for a program to take root and be successful you need people who believe in the approach and can commit to a common goal, upon my assignment as a coach; I looked for individuals that could also contribute to building and help the program reach its maximum potential. I found my partner in coaching, Sensei Reno. He was 60 years old, bold, with a great mustache. Sensei Reno was of Puerto Rican heritage but born and raised in the Bronx. Blessed with a great set of genes and an incredible physical discipline, Reno looked like he was 40. Reno and I shared training methodologies. He had worked at the Academy for many years, volunteering to teach Jujitsu to cadets during their free time mostly after 6 pm and on the weekends. He had competitive Judo experience as well and as I, he believed in the concept of developing leaders as fighters. He was denied the opportunity to help the Judo program by the previous coach because of his different training methods. However, I decided to bring him on board, and we agreed that together we would give the athletes the opportunity to become champions. "Every cadet an athlete" was a concept that we believed in wholeheartedly, and we were going to maximize our time to build these warriors.

Our team was small with only 14 athletes, two of them women. We started at aiming our training towards the Eastern Collegiate Judo

Association. The ECJA was an organization independent of the national level events, and our team had difficulty succeeding at this level mostly because most our athletes were in similar weight divisions and eliminated each other during the tournaments. During the second year of competition, we started to see some success with the men's team taking first place and the women's team taking second. At the national level, however, the competition was a different challenge as student-athletes in other universities were more experienced. Most our cadets had never done Judo, and they were participating at this level of national competition for the first time.

West Point provides competitive teams with an exceptional pool of physically talented athletes. What we could achieve during those first three years was a great start, and it was all due to their talent and ability to learn. These skills gave them an edge and provided them with the opportunity to taste some limited success at the national level. However, at that level, there were universities that provided scholarships for athletes, many of which came in as first-year students who were already nationally ranked black belt athletes. One prime example of this was San Jose State University. During my initial tour at the Academy, it was the most dominant team. All its athletes were nationally ranked, and they dominated the national collegiate program.

From 1998 until 2001, the West Point Judo athletes became more than just a club. They considered themselves cadets-athletes. On the training mat, they fulfilled their physical requirements, learned how to fight, and learned how to lead each other. I was very satisfied with that result. They were proud to be Army Judokas, becoming Eastern Collegiate Champions. They gave a tremendous effort in 2000 when the men came in third during the national championships. While I was happy for the athletes, I felt like we did not complete the mission. We wanted them to experience what it feels to be a national champion.

We wanted them to take down Goliath. We wanted them to win it all, but we ran out of time. The Army told me I had to move. Before I left in 2001, we arranged for Sensei Reno to stay in the program to prevent the team to return to the recreational mode that used to be on. I promised Reno and the team that I would return as a service member or as a civilian and that, we would complete the mission of becoming national champions.

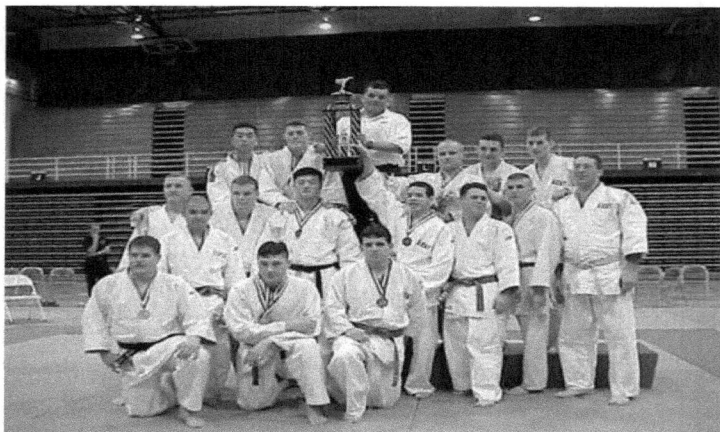

West Point Judo Team 2000 Eastern Collegiate Judo Champions

Chapter 4 – Pursuing Transformational Coaching

"You need to believe that there is a bigger plan. I am sure that you will get to coach them again. Trust the plan."

Maria S. Correa-Morales, My Wife,
As we Departed West Point in 2001

The Academy in the rear-view mirror is a sigh of relief for a graduating cadet, but I can safely say that it was not my sentiment as my family and I drove away in route to Fort Leavenworth, Kansas. That feeling in your stomach of leaving something incomplete was not one that I was used to, and it bothered me. Nevertheless, while my first tour at the Academy had just ended, I was grateful that it just opened the door to what I wanted to do as a coach and as a leader. That tour also exposed me to the teachings and approaches of Dr. Nate Zinsser at the Center for Enhanced Performance. As a coach, I tried to find the best way to reach my athletes and jumped neck-deep into sport and exercise psychology. I realized during those workshops that no team could succeed if it does not first set a foundation grounded in a realistic and motivational mental approach. This realization led me to further research transformational leadership and identify which elements can be transferred to coaching in sports settings. In transformational leadership, leaders create an environment that is designed to empower subordinates, create a motivational atmosphere, and develop cohesive teams that can unite behind a vision and a mission for the benefit of everyone in the team. All these elements can first be impacted by a strong mental approach.

After my departure from the Academy in 2001, every professional reading I did was associated with developing athletes mentally, learning how to provide them with strategies to dominate their mental skills, and maximizing their potential. I enrolled in a doctoral degree in sport and exercise psychology through Capella University with the aim of becoming a certified consultant through the Association for Applied Sports Psychology.

While in Kansas, I continued to expand my development as a coach. I traveled an hour to meet and watch Steve Scott run the Welcome Mat Judo Program. From him, I learned that coaches need to commit to an approach that is functional and that they believe in, and that an unwavering systematic approach will be more beneficial to the athletes in the end. He was Judo smart and had no issues going outside the institutionalized Judo mandates. Most importantly, his athletes were successful and enjoyed their training. Too many Judo and wrestling clubs run without a system, the approach to coaching is just what the Sensei or coach feels like teaching that day. That approach would not work at West Point, especially when we only have four years to produce a national level competitive athlete before they graduate and must move on to serve their country.

Following my tour at Fort Leavenworth, the Army assigned me to 2nd Infantry Division in Korea. During that tour, I continued my sports psychology education and had the privilege to join the Uijangbu City Judo Club and observe the coaches run a different program. In South Korea, instructors cannot have a Judo club if they did not graduate with a degree in physical education with a concentration in that martial art. The daily operations of that club reflected the coach's level of education. Their intensity was superb, but I also learned that the effectiveness of their program was connected to a smart recovery process that allowed athletes to reach their maximum potential. Many of the drills and activities that lead to the West Point Judo Team's success came from this extremely organized program.

Upon my return from Korea, my next assignment was to Fort Bliss, Texas. To continue my coaching development, I committed to complete the USA Judo Coaching Program and attended many of their coaching development sessions. All the new training approaches learned over the last two years since my departure from the Academy, combined with my experiences as an athlete under Sensei Tomita, Sensei Wilmer McNeese, and Karl Geis were implemented in the creation of the Fort Bliss Judo and Jujitsu Team in 2003. This team selected Soldiers from the installation and allowed them to train during the physical training segment of the day. Commanders supported this program, and that team had two competitors in each weight division for a total of 16 fighters. In 2004, the team won the Texas State Championships, and four athletes qualified to compete at the U.S. Senior Nationals. The program that was put together through research and commitment to the four pillars of performance: mental fitness, training, recovery, and nutrition, had its first successful trial run. I was committed to continually improving it and, hopefully, one day put into practice back at West Point. While many coaches could stay in one place and grow their programs, I had to do all the additional growing during my personal time, as my primary job was still to serve and protect our country.

In 2003, I was given the opportunity to coach the World Military Team that competed at the 3rd Military World Games in Catania, Italy. After having been on the roster as an athlete, the coaching opportunity gave me a new venue to experiment with my transformational coaching approach. I learned to connect with athletes at the individual level and to value their perspective when developing fight plans and mat side coaching methods. During those games, I met with each athlete individually to find out how to coach them during the competition. I recall Carlos Mendez, U.S. Air Force, telling me, *"Coach, I have been competing in Judo at the international level for over ten years and have never been approached by a coach to ask me that question. They always seem to have a plan in mind for me."*

I continued leading and coaching the Armed Forces Judo program for ten more years, taking the team to four more world military Judo Championships and their first international team win in over 20 years, meanwhile growing even more as a coach with every experience. At every international event, world-class athletes and coaches from multiple countries shared techniques and experiences in one of the greatest demonstrations of the Council for International Military Sports' (CISM) motto: "Friendship through Sports."

In the summer of 2002, the Army made the decision to terminate my field of work in short-range air defense systems. Because of it, I was sent to Fort Bliss that year to learn a new field as a high-altitude air defense officer. Caught in the crossroads of this Army decision, I stayed connected with my mission of developing Soldiers and leaders through the Army Combatives Program. At Fort Bliss, we were certifying around

100 Soldiers a month as combatives instructors. After one of my combatives graduation ceremonies, I leaned towards my wife and said, *"We are going back to West Point."*

She asked, *"When?"*

I replied, *"Soon. You were right, and I am trusting the plan."*

My future West Point athletes were just starting high school and probably making plans to compete for an assignment to the U.S. Military Academy, ensuring that they would stay on top of their classes as over 10,000 high school students apply for service academies each year, and a new class is only composed about 1,200 cadets. Judo was probably not part of their plans yet. None of them aware that a storm was brewing on the horizon, a storm that would impact all our lives and would connect us forever.

At West Point, Sensei Reno was holding down the fort, keeping the program competitive alongside great officers in charge such as MAJ Phil

Hughes, LTC Graylin Harris, and MAJ Ben Ring, passionate men who were emotionally connected, and that also wanted to make an impact in the Judo program.

Chapter 5 - Welcome to back to DPE. A Second Chance

"On behalf of the Dean of Academics and the Commandant of Cadets of the U.S. Military Academy, allow me to be the first to notify you of your selection as the next Academy Professor of Physical Education. Your passion for higher performance and cadet physical development was apparent in your interview. I look forward to working with you in the department for years to come. Welcome back to DPE."

Colonel Greg Daniels, Master of the Sword

The introduction to the combatives instructor certification course was coming to an end when I felt my phone vibrate in my pocket. It was a note from Dr. Sue Tendy telling me that the Department of Physical Education director was retiring and that soon they would begin the search for an academy professor for the department. I immediately made some calls to try to identify what steps needed to be taken to qualify and apply for this unique opportunity. The application packet was at the Academy in less than a week. I felt prepared for it because, since my departure from the Academy in 2001, I continued to contribute to Soldier and leader development and physical fitness. In Korea, I was the organizer of the Sports Festival for the Second Infantry Division, coached the basketball team, and helped in a Judo club in the civilian community. I returned to Fort Bliss and became a Master Combatives Instructor for the Army, certifying Soldiers to be leaders in the combatives program and to coach the Fort Bliss Judo and Jujitsu Team that offered Soldiers opportunities to compete. Also, I was coaching the Armed Forces Judo Team. I, therefore, felt strongly about the decision to apply as an academy professor.

It took almost a year for the Academy to complete the selection process. Over 50 officers applied for the position. I was excited when my name was among the top ten candidates, and they brought me to West Point for an interview with the search committee. My plan was to show my passion for the field, for the department, and for cadet development on all fronts.

My final statement to the search committee made an impact on their selection. I told them, *"It has been a great honor to be selected as a finalist for this academy professor position. I am confident that this board will recognize that I did not wake up one day, open the Army Times, saw an announcement and decided that this would be a nice job to do. I have been interested in and has worked towards becoming a physical education professional since I was 14 years old. I have done everything humanly possible, while still succeeding in my military duties, to be the most prepared individual for a position like this one. I am a successful military officer, a complete physical educator, and have made significant contributions to the Army in the areas that DPE teaches. I believe these elements are part of the job description for this position and I am ready to begin now."*

The Army combatives program had been introduced at the Army level and was spreading through the force. The timing for a combatives expert to instruct at West Point was right, and my passion for teaching and coaching was apparent.

The Army had selected Colonel Gregory Daniels as the new Master the Sword, the official title of the Department Head of the Department of Physical Education. In 2005, he notified me of the selection for the position. The announcement started a battle with my control branch to release me. However, the Military Academy was successful and ultimately got me to Florida State University to complete my Ph.D. in Sport and Exercise Psychology.

I arrived at the Academy in May of 2008 and served as the Deputy Director, a completely new role from my previous tour in DPE. In this new role, I had to opportunity to see things that I had not seen during my previous tour as a rotating military officer. I was surprised and even shocked by many of the decisions and leadership approaches taken at the higher levels at the

Academy. Nevertheless, I made it my mission to protect the department and continue to advance opportunities for the physical development for all cadets at the Military Academy. I returned to the Judo Team that first year as a part-time volunteer to assist in the program and the transition.

That summer was the arrival of the Class of 2012, the one we called the 50th Judo class. Major Ben Ring was the OIC of the Judo Program in 2008. He was in his last year, and that summer he asked me to assume responsibility for the selection of the program and the team, knowing that I would take over as the OIC upon his departure at the end of that academic year. The team was already 24 strong and competing very well. The Eastern Collegiate Judo Championships no longer existed, so they participated in tournaments in the Northeast region. Nothing had changed on the national level competitive scene since my departure in 2001. San Jose State was even stronger than they were before and had not lost in over ten years although West Point had come close several times to defeating them. The NCJA had now added novice divisions to the national championship. This new approach gave teams the opportunity to compete for four titles each year: advanced men, advanced women, novice men, and novice women. At the Academy, our primary focus was still winning the advanced divisions. That objective has been proven to be a difficult task for almost half a century, and it was in this division in which stronger teams have made their mark.

"Welcome to the Academic Year 2009 West Point Judo tryouts. My name is Lieutenant Colonel Hector Morales, and I will be the head coach of the West Point program during your stay here at the Academy. We are on a mission. This program started in 1962, and the men's team has not earned a national championship yet. You are the 50th-anniversary class, and you will be the first-generation of West Point Judo athletes who will be able to call themselves national champions."

The statement above was part of my initial introduction to the freshmen of the Class of 2012 in the summer of 2008. That group of young men and women felt the passion in the room, and they knew that we were about to do something special. The members of the Class of 2009, Class of 2010, and Class of 2011 that were already on the team also became extremely excited about the opportunity and the new training approach. From the beginning, they were all in, and they made that mission their own.

Meanwhile, we had requested an increase to 32 slots on the team to fix one of the biggest challenges we had. All the males on our team were almost in the same weight division, so we needed to create more even distribution among the weight classes. Then we went out to look for individuals to try out, and we selected into our program the members of the Class of 2012. Sensei Reno was still part of the program and very excited to be working together to accomplish what we had set out to do almost ten years before. We were back to helping these athletes reach their maximum potential and ensuring that they used that opportunity to grow.

During my second tour at the Academy, Dr. Ralph Pim led the sports program. Ralph was very much like me. He was passionate about the opportunities that the sports environment offers to develop men and women. He also believed that the program had the potential to provide great leadership tools to the cadet-athletes through the training, competition, and overall development. I worked closely with Dr. Pim to continue to create opportunities for all 27 sports in the competitive clubs' program. Unbelievably providing these opportunities for these programs was one of the biggest battles we had to fight at the Academy. It was challenging maintaining programs that were providing these opportunities to develop and compete because of the battle for time between the three developmental areas at the Academy: academics, military, and physical. As a student of the history of the physical program at West Point, I was not surprised to see resistance. Since the initial stages of the physical program during the early 1900s, COL Herman Koehler, the director at the time, wanted to provide cadets opportunities to compete and found himself battling with the academic board for support. Because I knew the value of these competitive opportunities, as the Deputy Director, I gave full support to the development of these programs. The competitive sports program skyrocketed during my period at the Academy and under Dr. Pim's leadership received accolades as one of the top 15 developmental sports programs in the nation. It was a perfect environment for the Judo Team to flourish, allowing us to continue our mission to provide those cadet-athletes with opportunities to represent the Army, themselves, and their families as well as to fight for a chance to one-day call themselves national champions. At times, for a vision to occur all-stars must be aligned. I believe that this was the case during this tour.

Sensei Reno and Sensei (LTC) Morales

Ready to Bring Change, Our Second Shot

(Photo Courtesy of BySoledad Photography)

Chapter 6 - Building a Team, Values that Matter

"My experience as a Judo player at West Point has fostered growth and strengthened my body and my mind to prepare myself better for the adversities that I will face as an officer and a Soldier. With the simple reinforcement of the warrior ethos and the additional duties presented to me on the team. I have loved every minute of my time spent on the mat. Judo has made me close friends and those I would consider family, with the beliefs of Judo to foster those relationships. The team has been a salient part of my growth here at the Academy. I cannot express how much Judo and this team have meant to me. I have also developed and grown in my technique and understand fighting, balance, mental strength as well as physical. I am a better fighter and a better person because of Judo. The hard work and countless hours of back breaking work along with the blood, sweat, and tears shed on the mat and in the dojo, have made bonds and relationships that will never be broken. Judo has changed my life."

Charles Bennett, Class 2012

Two Time Brigade Grappling Champion

Honor Graduate, Army Combatives Course

"Friday, we will have the final fight offs for the team that will represent the university at the national championships," Sensei Tomita said. *"Morales will fight Ocasio for the 189 pounds' spot. Be on time,"* he reminded us. As I prepared mentally to battle the reigning position holder, I reminded myself of the long hours of training, the additional runs, and the sacrifices made to earn that spot. I knew that there was a chance for me to lose that match but I was not going to let him have it. He was going to have to earn it.

Minutes before the match, my stomach was full of butterflies, and I was listening to the Vision Quest soundtrack, as it was customary during my preparation routine. The fight was a wrestling match with two periods of five minutes each. I had put in the time on the track, in the weight room, and on the mat. I was ready… the match started slowly for me as he came ready to finish me in the first minute. Before I knew it, the match was already 8-0 and the time in the first round was running out. During the short break, in between rounds, I looked up at my teammate and realized why he came at me so hard and why he wanted to win quickly. He was not physically ready to last the full ten minutes. He was gasping for air and visibly tired. His lack of stamina gave me a boost in confidence that fueled a very different second round. My plan was not to allow him to overpower me and stall for the next five minutes. I was relentless in my attack and kept coming for the entire round. The match ended 10-8 in my favor. He was much more experienced than me, but that did not matter that day. The lessons of this single match became the foundational values for every team that I was to coach in the future: warrior spirit, commitment, perseverance, and respect.

To win, you need to have a *warrior spirit*. That spirit influences your ability to compete. Without the willingness to take advantage of weaknesses in your opponent's preparation and plan you cannot succeed in a combative setting.

As we built the West Point Judo program, we looked for individuals with the willingness to fight. We looked for student-athletes with a background that exposed them to sports that instilled that competitive mentality. Athletes that grew up playing sports like hockey, rugby, jujitsu, and wrestling became our prominent targets because we knew that they would already bring that warrior spirit and we could mold them into high-level competitors. One such high-level competitor, Josh Sandhaus, came to the Judo team later in his West Point experience.

"I competed on the wrestling team for my first two years at West Point, mostly as the backup at 133 pounds' division but for several tournaments and duals, I was the starter, and it was a lot of fun. I left the wrestling team my junior year feeling disenchanted with the lack of cultivation and development that I and others were receiving. Leaving the wrestling team was one of the hardest decisions I had ever made. It was a sport that had been a part of my life since I was six

years old. It was and still is a part of the very
foundation of who I am as a person. It would not have
been an easy transition if I hadn't found Judo. From the
first day of practice, I felt welcome and part of the team.
It was a close-knit family with a strong work ethic and
motivating leaders. The success of the team can be
traced to the commitment of Sensei Reno and LTC
Morales, but you could feel the impact in each judoka.
I've been a part of a lot of teams during my career as a
high school and collegiate athlete and every winning
team always had one thing in common: a passionate
coach and empowered leaders."

> *Josh Sandhaus, Class 2011*

> *2011 NCJA National Champion*

> *2011 World University Team Selectee*

Another story of finding warriors was the
selection of Cadet John Barnes. John was a great
athlete and even a better fighter who was brought
in to Academy as a wrestler. Like Sandhaus, he
felt that the culture of the team was one that he
did not want to be part of. He chose to participate

in company athletics' combatives. During the finals of that tournament, Sensei Reno and I were watching the matches always looking to identify talent to continue to improve our team. We watched John toy with his opponent. He would take him down and then let him get up to just taking down again with some great foot sweeps and perfectly timed Judo throws. I turned to Sensei Reno, and I asked him, *"Did you see that?* He replied, *"I sure did."* Immediately after John's match, I called him to the side of the mat. John's recollection of that day is much better than mine.

"After competing in intramural grappling, or "slug athletics" as many cadets call it, I found success in submission fighting due to my roots in wrestling and judo as a kid. One day, I remember having a match in which I choked my opponent with a guillotine choke from my feet. After the match was over, the opposing coach was upset and was disputing with the referee whether my choke was legal. Immediately after the match, an officer dressed in a uniform from the West Point Department of Physical Education (the department that does not issue its staff members souls) point

at me and signal for me to approach him. My heart sank. I thought that I was about to be in a lot of trouble for my choke. However, I was relieved when the first thing that came out of the DPE instructors mouth was, "Have you ever done Judo before?" This was when I realized that he called me over because before choking my opponent, I threw him with a Judo move. I told the officer that I did, and he asked me to come out for the team. I asked if I could think about it and he replied, "absolutely not." I know that officer now as Lieutenant Colonel Morales, the head coach of the West Point Judo Team, and him noticing me that day changed my life."

> *John Barnes, Class 2013*
> *2011, 2012, and 2013 NCJA*
> *Medalist*

After warrior ethos, a high level of *commitment* was the second tenet of our core values. The day of my match at the University, I committed to leaving my heart on the mat. I convinced myself that even when the odds were against me, I was not going just to give it away. During our tryouts at the Academy, we had over

100 cadets competing for an average of 10 slots available on the team each year. All of them had enough physical talent to be added to the roster. However, we were more interested in their mental makeup than with their physical one. Building the physical was a lot easier than it was to make someone committed to the mission. I can recall the story of Cadet Catherine Clarke-Pounder. She wanted to be on the team but did not secure one of the slots during the tryouts. She worked so hard during tryouts that I wanted to give her a spot just to have an additional standard of effort present in the training hall. During tryouts, I would always save a spot for the hardest working athlete. I would tell that athlete that they would need to keep that intensity of effort if they wanted to stay on the team. That strategy paid off many times. With Catherine, the team was full of returning athletes, and I did not have that spot to give. A week went by after tryouts, and she kept showing up to practice and kept giving full effort in each

practice. In practice, I turned to Reno and asked, *"Didn't we cut her about a week ago?"* He replied, *"We sure did."* Nevertheless, there she was working out like that cut never happened. The next week an athlete became ineligible because of academics and we gave her the spot. Catherine went on to medal in several national championships and contributed greatly to the Women Team's successes.

There are many commitment stories from the athletes in our program, but one I remember well was the commitment of Spenser Donaldson to the higher requirements of the team. Spenser accepted a demotion from the roster and went on to compete in company combatives to provide his spot to a heavyweight athlete to makes us more competitive in our 2010 national title run. Spenser still came to the national event, won his novice division, and was a valuable member of the team contributing to our success in many ways during his West Point experience. He also graduated with his Judo black belt. Commitment is extremely important, and teams that want to be successful need to find creative ways to measure and recruit for it. We measured commitment based on the new candidates' willingness to stick to physically challenging experience and showing their grittiness.

When all is equal on the physical side, mental toughness will become the deciding factor because it has the potential to impact all other pillars of elite performance: quality of training, decisions that lead to improved recovery, and decisions that lead to proper nutrition and refueling. During the first two days of practice, the candidates participated in physical training activities we normally did during the training week. The mere exposure to these activities would weed out 60% of the individuals trying out. A practice that shows the expected commitment to the program will let you know how many of them want to pay the price. We asked for a commitment to the process, to their development, and to their teammates knowing full well that if all of them committed, the results would follow. Sometimes the desired results are not necessarily the victory of one athlete, but that they show the drive to gain victory, thereby motivating their peers to do the same. Ultimately, the team can be victorious even if the individual is not necessarily and individuals will find appreciation to the process in terms changing their definition of success.

"Although it was bitter losing my last finals match and never becoming a Collegiate Judo National Champion, I soon realized that being a part of the West Point Judo Team meant so much more than winning any match or any competition. Reflecting on this experience, I realized that even becoming a national finalist was outside of the reason I joined the team, and far from the reason I stayed on the team. Over two years later, I can look back and cherish all the things that made me join and stay on the team."

John Barnes, Class 2013

Three Time NCJA Finalist and Brigade Grappling Champion

Perseverance was probably the greatest lesson I took away from that qualifying match in college. If you are relentless in your approach, you are likely to achieve what you want. If you can put behind the challenges and perceived failures, you can look up and see the windows of opportunities that have just opened. It is no coincidence that most our athletes had a blue-collar type background in which hard work, dedication, and persistence were valued. The struggles that the team would go through and challenges the sport of Judo can present would require individuals that were willing to persevere. We made clear to all of them from day one that what we were about to attempt required a relentless approach and extraordinary efforts. We designed the training and competition schedule to reflect the challenges that they would face in competition to ensure that the actual tournament would feel easy.

"I wanted to thank you for the hard work ethic that you instilled in all the cadets and instilled the

notion of facing one's fears individually on the mat. I do not think I've ever had any experience quite like it, and I believe that this was mentally/physically more difficult than being in combat. In combat, I knew that I was with my platoon and that no matter what happened I had fellow Soldiers to be able to consult/console or fall back on. In Judo/wrestling, all that success was left on the mat, and I was individually responsible for my success/failure. There is a quote from Dan Gable that says, 'Once you have wrestled, everything in life is easy.' I truly believe that this applies to Judo as well. Since my departure, nothing has been on the same level of physical/mental pain. The strength and perseverance needed to get myself out of a pin/chokehold have been nothing quite like anything I have ever seen while in the Army."

Matthew Song, West Point Class 2009
2009 USA Judo Collegiate Champion

Respect was the last one of our core values. Respect is an important component of the Judo culture. We bow to the mat before we start training, we bow to the instructors before practice, we bow to our opponents before and after every match. However, we wanted more than that from that core value. Our culture required the student-athletes to believe and be fully in on something bigger than themselves. While they were pursuing three different paths on their journey: their academic degree, their military commission, and their Judo black belt, representing the Academy and the Army well was a top priority. We wanted our opponents to remember us as respectful competitors, but we also wanted to be respected for our passion and ability to play the game. We asked for a high level of respect in practice each day. That is where it all started for us: a deep respect for one another that required everyone, myself included, to leave our egos at the door for the benefit of the group.

"Respect and humility were an absolute necessity in the dojo. A lack of humility would cause you to tighten up and certainly get injured. Cadet Jung hit me with enough Drop Seoi Nage (shoulder throws)

to teach me that bringing my ego onto the mat was only going to cause me unnecessary pain. I learned to become loose and flow through moves better on the mat. I also learned that everyone around me has something to contribute to the betterment of the team and my personal Judo game. I learned Drop Seoi Nage (my go-to move) from Jung, footwork from Sandhaus and gripping techniques from Singley; the list goes on and on. Thanks to the climate in the Army Judo room, I take special care to understand where I am weak as a person and look at the people who surround me for support and guidance."

Joe McKenna, West Point Class 2013

An unwavering support of these four core values led to a solid foundation that could we could build upon. Our program was now 32 strong, with fighters in all weight divisions and every single one of them committed to the program goals, willing to persevere and embrace the challenges, while maintaining a competitive warrior spirit and a deep respect for the art, their teammates, and their mission. All ingredients of the recipe were in place; it was now time to cook.

Chapter 7 - The Will to Win Means Nothing
without the Will to Prepare

"Judo, the Gentle Way... or so they told us the first day of tryouts. It took about five minutes on the tatamis to realize that there was not going to be anything "gentle" about Judo. Having wrestled in high school and middle school, I expected as much entering my first year of West Point Judo, but what I did not expect was that it only got less "gentle" as the Hudson Valley winter swallowed our heating-less dojo to the point of which not even wearing your athletic socks kept the hard sting out of your toes. Jogging, rollouts, drills... Not even being "gentle" with your uke (partner) did anything to minimize the tingling in your side after a rough Ippon on the solid rock mat. The treacherous walk back up the ice-encrusted hill from practice to the barracks made you feel even more like a martyr."

Heather Purkey, West Point Class 2012,
2010 NCJA National Champion

Two years had passed since my last collegiate level competitive experience, and the glory days of the University of Puerto Rico Judo and wrestling teams were behind me. It was 1992, and I was posted at Fort Polk, Louisiana, as a platoon leader in the U.S. Army's 5th Infantry Division. The closest Judo club was one hour away in Beaumont, Texas. Therefore, my Judo Gi had now been hanging for almost two years. Finding the motivation to drive after a long day of work and balancing family seemed like an impossible task. I wished I could compete more but the willingness to find time for training was a different battle.

In the summer of 1992, my wife and I were watching the Olympic Games opening ceremonies on television. Watching the Puerto Rico delegation walk by the center of the stage was a special moment as I remember connecting emotionally with my desire to do more with Judo right away. The emotion was sparked by seeing my UPR Judo teammate Luis Martinez carrying the Puerto Rican flag. I was proud and extremely happy for him. That very moment reignited my will to train. A month later, I started driving to Beaumont twice a week and three hours to Houston, Texas twice a month on weekends for a higher-level training session at the Karl Geis Judo club. I began to compete for the Army and later qualified to attend the 1995 Armed Forces Judo Camp and Championships that would select the team to represent the U.S. at the First Military World Games in Rome. Making that team and earning the opportunity to represent the U.S. at those championships ingrained in me the belief that where there is a will, there is a way. That even when the light and fire within appear to be extinct, if you are passionate about what you do, there is still something there. This attitude is the same that I tried to reinforce in my athletes at West Point through exposure to a well-crafted set of goals, challenging training, and the promise of a unique experience.

"The beginning of my Yearling (sophomore) year coincided with the onset of a new era for the Judo team. We moved to a new dojo in Arvin gym, had LTC Morales as the head coach, and the outlook of the team was different since we were coming off USA Judo

Collegiate Championships. We began to receive more attention from West Point leadership and a large wave of people who were interested in trying out for the team. With new attention and talent, the new era of the Judo team included better-developed training, more tournaments, weight lifting and supplementary cardio training, and the creation of many more solid memories."

> *Sam Ellis, West Point Class 2012*
>
> *Team Captain 2012 Season, NCJA Silver Medalist*

The foundation of our competitive strategy was simple. First, we will not lose because of a lack of physical conditioning. Running out of gas in a match was not an option for us. We made up in fitness, explosiveness, mental toughness, and physical capability for the lack of Judo experience in our ranks. Our athletes understood from the first time they tried out that there was a significant physical requirement to be part of the team. Judo athletes need to have power and agility; they need to be flexible, and they need to possess the anaerobic capacity to last a five-minute match without visible signs of fatigue. They need to keep on coming throughout their entire match.

The physical aspect of our training included a balanced approach between the four pillars of performance: mental preparation, physical fitness, recovery, and nutrition. On the mental side, we trained aspects of mental/cognitive preparation each week and conducted progressive muscle relaxation on the last day of practice every other week. Athletes developed goals at the beginning of the season and tracked their performance throughout. For two seasons, one of the former members of the team, Travis Tilman became the team mental skills coach.

"Fighting with maintaining composure has been my strategy and has benefited me in winning competitions. Finally, although Judo training at West Point is not easy, it helps me become a better person and Soldier. I had to learn how to manage my time and overcome my potential complacency. In addition to

other requirements at West Point, such as military training and rigid academic study, Judo training makes me stronger and helps me build good character. Though I sometimes meet very good competitors, I have never wanted to quit. I try to learn something new and try as much as I can, which lead me to a better performance."

Sung-Won Jung, West Point Class 2012
Three-Time 81KG NCJA Medalist

The physical training portion included a meticulous weekly matrix that balanced high-intensity cardio, cardiorespiratory endurance, muscular strength, and muscular endurance with enough recovery for body adaptation. Also, athletes spent at least one and a half hour in the dojo (training room) developing their Judo specific skills.

The training also followed the principles of exercise and development that we upheld as law in the department of physical education: training progression, recovery, overload, balance, variety, individualism, and realism.

On the physical side, athletes recall progression through the Arvin Gym's stairway to Heaven. A set of stairs that ran from the basement to the fourth floor of the facility and that our athletes worked progressively from two repetitions at the beginning of the season in September to ten repetitions two weeks before the NCJA National Championships in March. Athletes disliked the progression, but the transferability to the mat and our first fundamental was superb and, after the fact, they appreciated it. It is a reminder to leaders and coaches that we do not have to enjoy everything we do to challenge our physical and mental systems and ourselves. The athletes will adapt and, in the end, will appreciate it.

Recovery was a top priority in our approach because of the demands of the military academy schedule. Also, my personal experience and injuries by wanting to do more as an athlete was explained many times to our cadets wanting to do more. The training plan included recovery and those who violated the rules of the recovery program placed themselves at risk of injury. As a matter of fact, some of the athletes who got injured admitted to not following the recovery plan. The best way for me to get buy-in from the cadet-athletes on the recovery strategy was to teach them that when you are resting is when adaptation occurs. That if there is no rest, the results will not show. For this population of athletes, this explanation seemed to take root. To aid in our recovery efforts, we asked to add a dedicated athletic trainer to our staff. In 2011, Katie Heckenbach joined the staff, and even when she also looked after other teams, she came to every training session, tournament, and national event. She took care of the athletes' immediate recovery and kept us informed of the athlete's status on our return to play protocol.

In our program, overload was a good thing. It was not to do more but to manage the intensity to force the adaptation. Many of the athletes came misunderstanding how to manage intensity in all four of the components of fitness: cardiorespiratory capacity, flexibility, muscular strength, and muscular endurance. The program allowed them to reach balance.

The principle of variety was implemented each week by providing athletes with different exercises that challenged specific areas of development. For example, stairs were replaced with interval work some Mondays. The idea was to work and improve the high-intensity cardio capacity system. Sometimes interval was running and sometimes was in bikes, sustaining the heart rate was the task, and we used multiple approaches to get to that end state while creating a training environment that was not predictable or boring.

Individualism and realism were observed weekly during the creation of training programs.

Athletes were encouraged to practice jujitsu, take combatives courses, and compete in combatives tournaments because these opportunities provided them with realistic application to their competitive training. Small adjustments in practice management led to individualism in training. For example, instead of asking the team to do 100 push-ups, our approach was for them to 2 minutes of push-ups to temporary muscle failure. This strategy allowed the athletes with a higher level of fitness to challenge themselves to improve and be the best they could be that day.

The nutrition pillar was taken care of for the athletes through the Academy. Their meals were provided throughout the day, and we kept track of those athletes making weight for competition. More than once, we pulled the plug on someone making weight because they were not progressing in a safe manner. Overall, we ensured the athletes were improving their physical fitness effectively and safely

"My Judo experience has provided me a tremendous opportunity for me to improve my physical fitness, be able to maintain calmness in facing challenges, and, most importantly, overcome my limits. Of course, as I keep practicing, I can feel that my physical condition is rapidly developing. My throwing and ground skills were refined through many practices."

Sung-Won Jung, West Point Class 2012
Three-Time 81KG NCJA Medalist

Another key fundamental to our fighting system was the expectation that we would not lose on the ground and would constantly improve our favorite and secondary standing techniques. While not consistent with Jigoro Kano's wishes of making the art purer by committing to the standing game, in Sports Judo, all elements of the game must be considered equally especially when your athletes lack the years of standing game that many of the experienced collegiate level athletes have. Out of the four ways to win a Sports Judo match, three of them are on the ground: submission by choke, submission by joint control, or a 20-second pin. Our athletes drilled and learned the transitions from the stand up to ground and all defenses available to repel ground submission techniques. We, however, wanted to win the match on the ground and learned multiple ways to finish the fight. When we heard other coaches tell their athletes *"Don't go to the ground with the Army guy,"* we knew that our system was working.

Lastly, we valued every match as a contributor to the team's success. Groundwork takes a significant amount of energy; therefore, proficiency in ground skills will lead to energy expenditure for the opponent and we knew that we had the gas to outlast that challenge. For example, an athlete may not win the tournament but if he can prevent his opponent from moving forward and sends him or her to the loser's bracket, their ability to pick up points for their team would decrease, giving us a better chance. More importantly, if we wore out our opponents in the early rounds of the tournaments, our teammates had a better chance to take advantage of their lack of fitness and win.

To support our second fundamental of our competitive strategy, improving our Judo skills and not losing on the ground, we had a sequence of development that allowed our athletes to complete a puzzle by the end of each training week. On Mondays, we would introduce two stand up techniques (throws). Tuesdays were dedicated to groundwork, instructing new techniques, and training ground fighting to include starting from positions that they did not like to increase their confidence to defend those holds or attacks. We placed them in all possible situations they could see in matches and tournaments. If we believed strongly enough that we would not lose on the ground and that we would end matches that went to the ground, we needed to give those techniques enough time to develop. On Wednesdays, we combined the two stand-up techniques we learned on the first day of the week and on Thursdays we tied up the transition of those combinations with the ground techniques for a complete set of transitions. If you understand your plan of attack and what your mission is, you will be able to find creative strategies to support your approach throughout the training.

The third fundamental of our winning culture approach was related to making sure every member understood that they were contributing to the team. While everyone sees Judo as an individual sport, in alignment with our competitive strategy, we saw it as a team effort. We sharpened each other; we showed up every day to make each other better and to ensure we were moving forward as a team. Each athlete committed to contributing to the overall results. If you bring your maximum effort to each match, your opponent, whether he wins or loses, has used a significant amount energy in that match, the energy that he or she will no longer have as they face one of your teammates in the finals. If we won each match and ended up fighting one of our teammates in the finals, which happened many times, there was no harm. Each of our athletes was expected to go out and give their max in every match. No excuses, no explanations.

"The Army fights and wins our nation's wars. There is no situation where an absolute victory by any means is acceptable to our nation's Army. In Judo, the same principle applied every time I stepped on the mat. Obviously, I didn't win every match I fought, but I contributed to my team and developed a warrior spirit through trial and error."

Joe McKenna, West Point Class 2013

2013 West Point Judo Physical Development Officer

Lastly, an important element of our approach was ensuring that the cadet--athletes felt a sense of home and family and that our dojo was a place where we could maintain an excellent balance between training and fun. I believe that you can be humble, be yourself, and at the same train hard to achieve great objectives. Judo is a tough sport by nature, cadet life at the Military Academy is a grind. Therefore, ensuring that the Judo environment was one that they looked forward to coming to every day was a top priority for me. In the dojo, we set the conditions for lifelong memories and connections.

"Being on the Team: the team was the best thing that happened to me while at West Point. It exposed me to new opportunities, helped me make lifelong friends (who also made dealing with West Point much more bearable), and most importantly, taught me about myself. Between cutting weight, winning and losing, and having different leadership roles on the team, I've grown as a military leader and a man. I could go on and on about all of the lessons, but in general, the team taught me to push through anything and everything."

Carson Giammaria, West Point Class 2014

2014 NCJA National Collegiate Champion

"My most fond memories while on the Judo team were not necessarily in competing but rather the celebrations that would occur before and after practice. Every once and a while for no reason people would start to dance. Someone would put a new song on the speakers and slowly but surely everyone would start to move. No inhibitions, no judgment; just future Officers in the world's most powerful Army dancing their hearts out. People would be backflipping off walls, showing off fancy footwork, and laughing and celebrating life, and the camaraderie of the team. There was never a dull moment on the Judo team and all time not spent sweating or practicing was spent joking, and laughing, and dancing. I have never met a group of harder working, dedicated, and hysterical men and women in my life, and I will treasure the memories I shared with them forever."

Patrick Cronin, West Point Class 2013

2013 Team Captain, NCJA Finalist, and
Medalist

"Every practice has become more than an escape
from the grind of the pressure cooker, of the Academy —
it is going home at the end of a long day, where we
don't have to worry about drama, our next exam, or
getting a hug. It's entering the steel cage to release
frustrations without anyone holding it against us. It's
fighting alongside our brothers and sisters in imagined
engagements. It's praying at the sacred temple with
sweat running down our backs. It's West Point Judo,
and we call it family.

West Point Judo grew even more over the
following years and with it a profound sense of pride
and family. Each day we came to practice knowing very
well what was in store: maybe a Reno Surprise, or a
ridiculous circuit planned by Sensei Morales, or a
gruesome death by lactic acid during sprints up the
Stairway to Heaven. But we also came with the
understanding that you put your all in for the people
and coaches that surrounded you, for the solemnly

humbling group of hard workers that were quick to throw you but even quicker to pick you back up."

Heather Purkey, West Point Class 2012

NCJA National Champion

Chapter 8 – Taking Down Goliath

"What everyone expected least of all, however, was to take first place at NCJA Collegiate Nationals, usurping San Jose for the first time in American Judo history. San Jose State was shocked most of all, especially given the kaleidoscope of mat experiences our small team boasted on a good day. Looking back, it should not have been so surprising. We were a hard-working team under the new guidance of LTC Hector Morales, who had succeeded along with the Yoda of Judo, Sensei Reno, in recruiting possibly the largest group of freshmen the team had ever seen."

Heather Purkey, West Point Class 2012

2010 NCJA National Champion

When I left the Military Academy in 2001, the athletes gave our family a cadet sword as a memento of our time spent together on the team from 1998-2001. This sword has been hanging in our living room ever since. Every time I glanced at it, I remembered the times we spent together, the individual accomplishments, and how that group of men and women went from a club to a team, from cadets to cadet-athletes, and how proud they were about their performance. However, I also thought often about how close we came to the national title. We came in on third place in 2000, and I knew that with two more years, it could have happened. As we drove away from West Point in 2001, it was uncertain if I would ever get the opportunity to go after them again. However, as my wife cleverly pointed out, there is a bigger plan and second chances do exist. Our chance was here now. Academic Year 2010 was full of promises with several athletes who picked up the sport quickly and were eager to win. Also, the business of taking down San Jose State at Nationals was no longer just my mission. You could feel it in the dojo, and we were all in.

At the beginning of the 2010 Academic Year, our team roster was locked in. We had at least two athletes in each weight division, and they were all connected with our plan. We recruited two former division one wrestlers and a former rugby player, Andrew Fant, one of the most talented athletes I have witnessed in the sport. Andrew became a USA Judo Collegiate Champion the previous season, and in the fall of the 2010 academic year, he earned points in the USA Judo National Roster at the Dallas Invitational, one of the toughest tournaments in the U.S.

For that year, we laid out the plan and the goals for the team:

Team Goals AY 2010

The 2009-10 West Point Judo Team will:

- Win the NCJA National Championships

- Beat Navy and Air Force

- Place at least one cadet on the USA Judo National Roster

- Certify at least 5 Judokas Level 1 Combatives Instructors

- Certify at least 5 Judokas as Regional Referees

- Be in the top third of the competitive teams in Academic Performance Score, Military Performance Score, and Physical Performance Score.

- Average Army Physical Fitness Test (APFT) Average Score of 270

By the end of December 2009, all goals except the NCJA Championship and the year performance scores were already accomplished. We defeated Air Force 11 matches to 1 and defeated Navy 20-0. Andrew Fant placed at the Dallas Open and earned points for the USA Judo National Roster. The Fall APFT gave us the above 270 score that we were after. The first-semester combatives course gave us seven certified instructors and a referee clinic helped our senior athletes understand a bit more about rules and refereeing. We were now aiming towards the National event at Texas A & M and our most challenging goal of the year.

After we had returned from the Winter break, Andrew Fant was waiting for me in the dojo. *"Sir, I am ready to go, I want to compete at Nationals,"* he stated. Andrew had suffered a severe concussion at the end of the previous semester that challenged his short-term memory. We knew that he was a very talented athlete, one of the best we have ever seen and that the doctors had cleared him to participate, which is what made the decision difficult. This decision was one of the most challenging experiences of my coaching career because the athlete wanted to compete and, somehow, was cleared by the medical team. However, I was aware that as a former rugby player, he also had several previous concussions. I knew that we needed him to compete if we wanted to accomplish our goals. If he placed first, he would contribute team points at the event. Nevertheless, without hesitation, I explained to him that I could not allow him to compete. He was visibly upset, but I was able to explain to him how important his commissioning was to me and why I was not willing to gamble with his future.

"Andrew, you are a great athlete, but you are going to be a better leader," I recall telling him. *"Your contributions to the Army will be far more than what we can use from you here this year. Please stay and help me in an admin role. Be a part of the team without competing. Everyone knows your character and your ability to fight; no one will be questioning that."*

"Yes, sir, thank you," he said and walked away from the dojo never to wear a Judo Gi again.

An athlete like Andrew is difficult to replace. He was our heavyweight, a natural athlete above 220 pounds that was very rare at the Academy where the average weight for male athletes was around 180 pounds. The only other athlete I have seen that could fill his spot was in the most unexpected place at the Academy.

One of my other athletes, Charles Bennet, had requested permission to participate as part of the rabble-rousers during the first semester as that squad needed strong men that could assist with the acrobatics to cheer on the crowd. As part of the squad, there was a possible candidate to take the heavyweight division. In January, when Charles came back and asked me to get back on the team, I paused for a second and said, *"I am not sure, things are tight right now, and the team is focused for Nationals. I need to talk to the cadets in charge, and I will let you know"*. Charles is like a son to me, there was no doubt that he was going to be back on the team, and he knew this because he had an extensive background in ground fighting. Nevertheless, it was a good opportunity for me to get him to help the team by bringing the other rabble-rouser on board. *"Charles, if you convince Kyle to join the Judo team, you are in for sure,"* I told him. He smiled and went out to search for our heavyweight contender. Kyle was also a great athlete, former wrestler and football player who had the makeup needed to learn Judo defense quickly and at least several combinations that would allow him to contribute some points to the team score. I did not expect him to win, just to place and not give San Jose or any of the other schools easy points. I immediately enrolled him in the elective basic Judo course, and he started to attend the team practices in the afternoon.

In April 2009, when West Point Judo won the USA Judo Collegiate Division at the National Scholastics Championships, the taste was bittersweet because their primary rival and one of the most dominant schools in the nation, San Jose State University, was not present. San Jose State University, which has a varsity program that mostly brings freshmen black belts to their school, has been the prominent leader in collegiate Judo for 48 years, and the team had never been defeated over the last decade. The San Jose State's leader is an icon in American Judo, Mr. Yosh Uchida. He is well known, highly respected, and what he has done in that program and the number of student-athletes he has developed is admirable. Defeating

San Jose appeared to be impossible for any program that only had developmental Judo athletes, and that is why it appealed to the members of my team, Sensei Reno, and to me.

In March 2010, at Texas A & M, West Point Judo athletes made history in collegiate Judo by rendering San Jose State their first team defeat in a long time as well as placing ahead of 25 other colleges and universities represented at the event. West Point Judo athletes had been preparing for this moment for two years, they understood who the biggest rival was, and they knew that they needed to find ways to take them out of the competition early.

In the Judo competition system, once you lose a fight, you are out of the gold and silver medal rounds. For team points, the system allows for 5 points for first place, 3 points for second place, and 1 point for 3rd place. However, if a team places more than one athlete in the top three of the same weight division, only the highest placed athlete collects points.

During the first round of competition at the 2010 National Collegiate Judo Championships, West Point Judo 66kg fighter Josh Sandhaus (Class 2011) and team co-captain 73kg Dan Diccico (Class 2010) faced two experienced black belts from San Jose State University. Both extraordinary athletes made a significant contribution to the team's final score by defeating the San Jose State athletes getting them out of gold and silver medal contention right from the start. Sandhaus, a new member of the team that season and a green belt, threw for Ippon one of the most experienced black belts in the tournament while Diccico managed to out-grip his opponent to frustration to the point that he was disqualified for receiving three penalties.

At the 60kg division, sophomore Arthur Lin (Class 2012) secured the bronze medal after four grueling matches. The cadets dominated the 66kg Division when senior Nathan Horswill (West

Point Class 2010) swept the division to become a National Collegiate Judo Champion. Sophomore Samuel Ellis (West Point Class 2012) took second at the 66kg also defeating every contender very convincingly in his bracket until he faced his teammate in the gold medal match. Sophomore Jung Sung-Won (West Point Class 2012) secured the silver on the most heavily populated 81KG division. Senior David McCurdy (West Point Class 2010) placed 3rd in the same division after winning three fights in a row in the consolation bracket.

In the 90kg division, newcomer Junior Anthony Adez (West Point Class 2011), who was also only a green belt, surprised two black belts on his way to the gold medal match. On the gold medal match, he faced an international player from the University of Colorado at Colorado Springs. Adez loss the match but brought home the silver on his first national collegiate Judo appearance. In the 100kg division, Sophomore

Patrick Singley (West Point Class 2012) won all his preliminary matches to gain an appearance at the gold medal match versus a black belt from Idaho State University. Cadet Singley, fighting one division above his weight class, defeated black belts and fought an extraordinary match in the gold medal round. He also brought home the Silver. Senior Kris Kilgroe, after a tough loss in the second round of the preliminaries, fought his way on the consolation bracket to get another bronze medal for the cadets denying points to any other program in that division. In the heavyweight division, Sophomore Kyle Schlauch (West Point Class 2012), a true newcomer to Judo, defeated all his opponents to become a National Collegiate Champion on his first national level appearance. CDT Schlauch replaced national level athlete, Junior Andrew Fant who could not participate in the event because of an injury. West Point Judo athletes placed in every division except the 73kg to collect a total of 20 points versus 13 points collected by San Jose State who took second in the senior men category. A true team effort to bring home West Point's first-ever NCJA Advanced Men's National Title.

With only five athletes competing at the advanced female division, the West Point Women's Judo team took second place to the San Jose State team. Performances lead by Sophomore Heather Purkey (West Point Class 2012) who after losing her first match, collected four impressive wins and became the first women in the new West Point Judo era to become an individual Collegiate National Champion. Heather defeated all athletes a division with 5 or more competitors. Senior Nargis Kabiri (West Point Class 2010) also defeated everyone in her division contributing to the team's second-place finish. Sophomore Ariel Espinoza-Levy brought home the silver medal in the 57kg division while Freshman Katherine Donohoe and Catherine Clarke-Pounder brought two bronze medals in the 57kg and 70kg weight divisions respectively. The West Point Judo

Program's goal became to increase women participation in this warrior ethos building sport and defeat the San Jose University women's team. West Point Women's Judo Team showed promise, and we became more confident that they would develop into a National Championship team in the very near future.

Five athletes competed at the Novice division where West Point also took second place. Sophomores Charles Bennett and Spencer Donaldson took the gold in their respective divisions. Senior Kabiri who also fought the novice division also won the gold. Junior Michael Gibson won three matches to secure silver as well as freshman Catherine Clarke-Pounder who also took second. Freshman Ryan Wilson brought home the bronze.

We had done it! One of our four teams became a National Champion. The question now was, where do we go from here? How can we continue to move the bar up for athletes to feel challenged? The answer: shifting our focus and aiming to take it all!

West Point Judo's First Men's Team National Title in 49 years.

Chapter 9 - Redirecting Goals, Winning it All

"When I deployed to Afghanistan in 2013, I ran into two of my former Judo teammates – Spencer Donaldson and Matt Song. In fact, I spent several days at Camp Leatherneck with Spencer Donaldson, and on several occasions, we reminisced about times on the Judo Team. We laughed about the time we elected to go to Puerto Rico with the Judo Team over Spring Break, thinking that we would be spending more time partying on the beach rather than training in a dojo. Boy, were we wrong. We spent most of that week in a dojo, being manhandled by the dominant Puerto Rican Judo Team. Despite having a sober spring break, we left with a deeper knowledge of the sport and unbreakable friendships like the one I have with Spencer."

Art Lin, West Point Class 2012

Three-Time NCJA Bronze Medalist

"Congratulations! All of you, our newest national collegiate champions, have been invited to a special training camp," Sensei Tomita said. I was excited about this training opportunity. When we got to the training site, we saw the entire national

team on the mat. There were much older individuals with proven international competitive experience and us, young collegiate level athletes eager to learn. That was one of the most difficult and challenging training experiences in my life. Each day during that camp I left the mat smoked and burned out. On the way back, Sensei Tomita said something I would never forget. *"We should never think that we have arrived."* At that moment, I understood the intention behind the invite. Success can cloud the mind of a young athlete; a reality check is a great tool to motivate you in your journey. I have thought about this statement throughout my entire career and have used it as a self-check mechanism. Every time I started to feel comfortable, I looked for a change of direction for another area to improve. Now that we had reached our over a four-decade-old goal of winning a National Championship, this approach was more needed than ever. The Puerto Rico trip described above was not a coincidence, and I believe athletes appreciated it, after the fact of course. We needed to revitalize our goals and our approach to keep the cadet-athletes challenged and focused.

While our goals were very similar regarding areas, we pushed the envelope to challenge the team in a different way. In 2011, our primary goal was to win all the divisions at the NCJA Championships. This task has never been accomplished at the National Collegiate Judo Association since the establishment of the novice division in the early 2000s. We wanted to beat Navy and Air Force and to place at least three cadets on the USA Judo National Roster, an increase from one the previous season. Also, we wanted to expand our horizons by competing in the Navy Sponsored Commandant's Trophy and Japanese Ambassador's Cup tournaments. These events were open to clubs outside of the collegiate program, and we successfully defeated older and experienced players taking both awards home and retaining them for three seasons.

"On the mat, I have one memory that stands out above all the rest: The Army-Navy judo match in 2011. This match was one of the most intense sporting events I have ever been a part of. The energy in the room was extremely high. Both teams cheered their lungs to death as Navy tried to dig down in a couple of close matches to preserve a couple of shreds of dignity. The most exciting and rewarding part was seeing a couple of our younger guys like Pat Diehl win against Navy's experienced guys in close matches. Additionally, it goes without saying that our more experienced guys and girls crushed their average guys and girls. I'll never forget how loud and intense the competition got in that small venue. What an incredible memory."

Sam Ellis, West Point Class 2012

Team Captain 2012 Season

To continue one of our other goals, to grow leaders for the Army Combatives program, we set out to certify at least five Judokas as Level 1 and Level 2 Combatives Instructors. We wanted to certify five Judokas as regional referees and to reach a 270 average in the APFT. By February 2011, our goals accomplished, our teams were ready for the national championship. After the 2010 success, I requested an increase in our athlete membership to ensure our team had enough players in each division to complete quality training and to sharpen each other throughout the year. This request became an elevated battle with the commandant of cadets' staff who wanted more cadets on the marching field in the afternoons and less in competitive activities, the same battle fought almost a century before by Colonel Herman Koehler, the father of physical education at West Point. It was a battle that I was honored to have in common with that icon of physical education and one which I decided not to back down from. I strongly believe that what those cadets gained from their competitive training experiences in the afternoons surpassed any lessons they would learn on the marching field. Also, if we wanted to grow novice and women's programs, we needed those additional slots. After several months of frustration, our request was finally approved, and our team was given eight more slots for a total of 40 cadet-athletes. We were now able to build full women's and novice teams, giving us a better chance to accomplish our goals for the year. We now had the biggest team in the history of the West Point Judo program.

Throughout the 2011 Academic Year, the cadet-athletes were exposed to high caliber training and physical development. To continue to develop and keep the team motivated, we brought world class coaches and athletes to share techniques with our athletes. Sensei Tomita and my UPR teammate, Hiram Cruz, gave clinics at West Point. Some of our athletes were also exposed to the training approaches of Leo White, USA Judo Olympian and the most successful USA Military Judoka. Bringing other experts in the field whom I share training philosophies with was designed to reconnect the athletes with our training approach, sustain their motivation, and for them to hear the message from a different voice.

"This is the day we have been training for. All those hours of training, all the sweat, all the tears were spent to build what you needed to be successful today. I want you to fight your heart out; I want your opponents to wake up trembling and sweating in the middle of the night because they are having a nightmare about the day they fought an Army Judoka. I want them to tell their grandchildren about their worst day on the mat as a Judo athlete, the day that they entered our house and tried to take away our championship. Represent the Army, your family, and yourself. Make us proud, make history."

Sensei Morales' Opening Remarks to the Team in 2011 NCJA Championships.

On Saturday, 12 March 2011, West point Judo made history again, this time by winning all the divisions at the National Collegiate Judo

Championships, a first-time accomplishment in US collegiate Judo history. Competing in front of a home crowd at the Cadet Physical Development Center in Arvin Gymnasium, the cadets fought with amazing tenacity and passion, determined to prove that their victory in the Men's division the previous year over rival and perennial powerhouse San Jose State was not a fluke. They succeeded in doing so and established themselves as a new dominant force in collegiate Judo.

The competition consisted of Judo athletes representing 33 different colleges and universities and was noted by Chuck Jefferson, the President of the National Collegiate Judo Association, as one of the toughest he could remember. The stakes were higher than normal in the competition this year. First and second place finishers would earn points towards qualification for the USA Judo National roster, and all first-place finishers would be asked to represent the United States at the World University Games in China that August.

However, the West Point Judo team could rise to the occasion with 33 out of 39 cadets who competed in this tournament placing and walking home with a medal.

The Men's Advanced Team's success was led by the heroic efforts of senior brown belt Joshua Sandhaus (West Point Class 2011). Josh faced down favored black belts from San Jose State and Boston College before defeating West Point's own John Barnes (West Point Class 2013) in the finals to win the 66kg men's division. Incredible performances also delivered by junior Sun-Wang Jung (West Point Class 2012), second place in the 81-kg, and senior Josiah McCoy (West Point Class 2011) who also placed second in the 100-kg division. Freshman white belt Justin Adkins (West Point Class 2013) who against all the odds finished second in the over 100 kg division. Junior Art Lin (West Point Class 2012) rounded out the men's team point winners with a third-place finish in the 60-kg division. The combined efforts of these individuals earned West Point a team score of 15 which put them in front of San Jose State who only mustered six team points. Third place shared between Idaho State and UC Berkeley, each of which earned five team points.

The Women's Advanced Team showed true dominance over their competition with first-place finishes from freshman Juliet Talavera (West Point Class 2014) at 48kg, sophomore Larisa Tudor (West Point Class 2013) at 70kg, and freshman Kristen Hernandez (West Point Class 2014) in the over 78kg division. The women's team also benefited from second place finishes from sophomores Katherine Donohoe (West Point Class 2013), Catherine Clarke-Pounder (West Point Class 2013), and team co-captain Danielle Munoz (West Point Class 2011). Junior Heather Purkey (West Point Class 2012) and freshman Elizabeth Posey (West Point Class 2014) earned third place finishes in the 63kg and 70 kg divisions which added to the team's first-place finish as well. The women's team faced their toughest competition from Iowa State and Texas A & M which finished 2nd and 3rd respectively. Both men's and women's novice teams also finished in first place to complete the team's sweep of team national championships.

2011 West Point Judo Team at Arvin Cadet Physical Development Center after the 2011 NCJA National Championship Sweep

(Photo Courtesy of BySoledad Photography)

Celebrating the 2011 Championships

(Photo Courtesy of BySoledad Photography)

Chapter 10 - From the Mat to the Field, Leadership Lessons that Transfer

Behind the competitive experience of our program at West Point is the transferability of what we did on the mat and as members of the team to the cadet-athletes' development as leaders. Below you will see how the West Point Judo experiences influenced their leadership approach and how they connected the lessons learned in our program.

"I know now that great leaders access people's potential by allowing them the freedom to try, by empowering them, and by making them believe in the mission. This allows them to succeed. Demanding success from people is a sure path to failure."

CPT Nate Horswill, Class 2010

2010 NCJA 66 KG National Champion

"The mentality of a Judo athlete is unlike any other and can be a powerful tool in every aspect of a

person's life whether it be through study, interpersonal relationships, or in my chosen career as an Army Officer. Coupled with my experience at West Point, I can think of nothing that could develop me better mentally, physically, or emotionally. Graduating West Point with a Commission in the US Army, a Diploma from the United States Military Academy, and a Black Belt under LTC Morales will be the greatest accomplishment of my life thus far."

1LT Pat Cronin

2013 NCJA Nationals Medalist

"I am proud to be a member of the West Point Judo team. I have learned: first that if we do not give up in the face of challenge we will only grow in our abilities; second that the support system that surrounds us, in this case, my team and my coaches, can make a big difference in our development as players and as leaders; and finally I know that we are lifelong learners and Judo is not an exception, no matter how much you think you know, if you have an open mind you will

realize how much more you have to learn . This last lesson was reinforced to me every day at practice, competition, clinics or common training with other teams, there is always some variation or some technique that somebody does that I have never seen before. I will always do my best to represent the West Point Judo team and all the values that it stands for not only within the academy but also everywhere I go."

1LT Larisa Tudor

2011 NCJA 70 KG National Champion

1st Romanian Woman to Graduate West Point

"As an Infantry officer, it is my job to orchestrate fire and maneuver. Using a Platoon of 35-40 men, I create a tactical dilemma for the enemy where they are presented with two or more equally bad courses of action. This is the same thing I tried to do as a Judoka. I made sure my opponent knew no matter what step they took, my Ippon was coming."

1LT Joe McKenna

2013 Physical Development Officer

"Fast forward two years, and I am now stationed at Fort Hood, Texas. I am an Army Aviation Platoon Leader in the 1st of the 227th Attack Reconnaissance Battalion, 'First Attack.' So much of the qualities that I learned and practiced as a member of the West Point Judo Team apply to my job today. I practiced patience in fitting in with everyone when I first joined the team. This is a quality that I practiced as a new platoon leader, arriving at a new unit as the new guy that nobody knew and learning how to play my role in a company that already had its rhythm before I arrived. I practiced persistence and determination as a Judoka when I learned and perfected new moves that are effective at the collegiate Judo level. This is a quality that I use every day, in learning to become a more effective warfighter surrounded by combat veterans. One of the most important things I practiced, though, was camaraderie. At West Point, I was surrounded by a team I would go to the extremes for. This is a relationship I believe every soldier should have with his or her unit."

1LT John Barnes

3-Time NCJA Finalist and Medalist

"Judo was such a big part of my life that I've
continued to train in MMA, joining a few clubs, and
participating in some competitions. I also went to the
Master Combatives Course where I graduated as an
honor grad. Most recently, though, I've had to fall back
on the lessons I've learned from the team to deal with
the obstacles at Ranger School. There's not a single day
there that I can't draw parallels to my experiences at
West Point and with the team."

2LT Carson Giammaria

2014 NCJA 66 KG National Champion

"During my four years on the team, I learned a
lot and made a ton of awesome memories. All my
experiences on the team certainly added to my
development as a person. I learned the patience and
control that comes with learning Judo, as well as the
hard work that comes with the training. I'm sure these

attributes played into my success at the Academy, along with any success since."

CPT Sam Ellis

2012 Team Captain and NCJA Silver Medalist

"After I graduated the Academy and began my military career, I stopped doing Judo. My excuse was that I was too tired after the long days to get beat up in the dojo, but the truth was that I missed my team. I missed the laughter, the comradery, working towards an inspiring goal with like-minded hard workers. The platoon I had just recently taken over wasn't a team either due to a myriad of factors. I wanted my team. Since my team was scattered to West Point and the four winds, I pledged to use the same fundamentals we used as part of West Point Judo to build the team towards a mission in my platoon. Even though I only had a year with them, I was proud that when I left, they were working hard and growing together to complete our mission more efficiently. They had the special characteristics that make a group a team: a positive

group identity, trust to leverage each other to solve problems, laughter in the face of adversity, respect for one another... They had become my team. While I in no way could have steered them to reach their full potential by myself, I know that had I not used my experience on the Judo Team and set the example, the platoon would have continued to suffer the apathy, mistrust, and disorganization that prevented it from achieving its mission to the fullest, from being a team."

Heather Purkey, West Point 2012

2010 NCJA National Champion

Chapter 11 - Epilogue – A Positive Culture Can Generate Change

"I have never been in a more hostile environment that in the 2012 National Collegiate Championships at San Jose State. It was a tense environment for us as coaches and for our athletes. But I guess this is the price of change and of being on top."

Reno Claudio, Coach West Point Judo Novice Team

The West Point Judo Team achieved some unexpected results in both the 2010 and the 2011 seasons and continued to develop until my retirement in 2014. West Point Judo's success impacted change in other programs. San Jose brought in a full-time coach and doubled up on their recruiting efforts, and by 2012 they were ready to regain their titles. At Collegiate National in San Jose in 2012, the environment was challenging as everyone was in to support their athletes defeating West Point and getting their place back at the top level of collegiate Judo. San Jose has always been a great program, but we could challenge their dominance with a team without much Judo experience, doing what no one else could do. In 2012, San Jose regained the advanced men division by six points and West Point Judo retained the Advanced Women, and both novice divisions.

At Collegiate Nationals, the battle for dominance continued over the next two years as in 2013 and 2014, West Point took home five out of the eight contested divisions. The 2013 team retained Navy Commandant's Trophy, the Japanese Ambassador's Cup, defeated Air Force and Navy and won both novice national level divisions. The 2014 team repeated the same feats and regain the Advanced Division Women's National title led by the stellar performance of Carly Patton and Elizabeth Posey who both took gold. Sarah Goodman, Rachel Oliver, Ciara Gerald, and Tiara Hansen who took silver, and Juliet Talavera, Pearl Brooks, and Sara Roberts who earned bronze. The Men's Team Captain Carson Giammaria became the 66kg National

Champion with a flawless performance to led his team to a second-place finish. Other great performances by male medalists on the final tournament include Kyle Underwood and Richard Mendoza who won silver medals and Peter Stanley, Austin Bowman, Stephen Patton, and Patrick Diehl who earned bronze medals. The 2014 Collegiate National Championships at Texas A & M was my last as the coach of the West Point Judo team and we had a medal winner in each of the 16 advanced categories, a great contrast to the zero medals in 16 categories on my first year as coach of West Point in 1998.

West Point Judo athletes went to serve their country and have been deployed all over the world in Afghanistan, Korea, Iraq, Kuwait and many other locations. These young men and women of character have taken their championship experience into their leadership approach and are making an impact in the world.

I retired after 26 years of military service and left the academy to join the mental conditioning team of the Pittsburgh Pirates organization where I have the privilege and opportunity to continue to work and challenge athletes and coaches to help them reach their maximum potential.

The West Point Judo team accomplished some unexpected and incredible things on and off the mat. They changed the perceptions that the Academy had of the of Sport of Judo, set personal records, and, in the process, became warriors. Regardless of where we are, we have our competitive years, our memories, and that feeling inside that tells us that regardless of the difficulty of the task, we can accomplish it because we are champions.

Cadet Charles Bennett - Graduation Class 2012

(Photo Courtesy of BySoledad Photography)

50th West Judo Team

50th West Judo Team (Customary Fun Photo)

Chapter 12 - West Point Judo Accomplishments from 2009 - 2014

-2009 -

USA Judo Scholastics Championship

NCJA Advanced Men 3rd Place

-2010 –

NCJA Advanced Men's Team National Championship, 2nd Place Advanced Women's Team, 2nd Place Novice Men, 2nd Place Novice Women

- 2011-

NCJA Advanced Men's Team National Champions, Advanced Women's Team National Champions, Novice Men National Champions, Novice Women National Champions

- 2012 –

NCJA Advanced Women's Team National Champions, NCJA Novice Men National

Champions, NCJA Novice Women National Champions, 2nd Place - Advanced Men's Team

-Navy Commandant's Trophy and Japanese Ambassador's Cup

- 2013 –

NCJA Novice Men National Champions, NCJA Novice Women National Champions, 2nd Place - Advanced Women's Team, 2nd Place - Advanced Men's Team

-Navy Commandant's Trophy and Japanese Ambassador's Cup

- **Katherine Donohoe** is Awarded the GEN Hal Moore's Warrior Athlete of Excellence Award

- 2014 –

NCJA Advanced Women's Team National Champions, NCJA Novice Men National Champions, NCJA Novice Women National Champions, 2nd Place - Advanced Men's Team

- Beat Air Force - Six Times

- Beat Navy - Nine Times

- **Cadet Katie Loss** - is Awarded the GEN Hal Moore's Warrior Athlete of Excellence Award

- From 2009 until 2014, West Point Judo athletes individually collected **57 gold**, **37 silver**, and **24 bronze** medals at the National Collegiate Judo Association Championships.

- 19 Cadet-athletes Became NCJA Advanced Division National Collegiate Champions.

- 34 Cadet-athletes became NCJA All-American by placing 1st or 2nd at Nationals and earned points in the USA Judo National Roster.

- Sensei Reno received the Coach Mike Krzyzewski's Teaching Character through Sports Award in 2009.

- Sensei Morales was named NCJA Coach of the Year in 2010 and 2011 and USOC Developmental Coach of the Year for Judo in 2013

- Sensei Morales received the Coach Mike Krzyzewski's Teaching Character through Sports Award in 2014.

Appendix I – West Point Judo Team Rosters, Captains, and All-Americans Academic Years 2010 - 2014

AY10 Men's Team

NAME	CLASS	Div
ADEZ, ANTHONY**	2011	73kg
BENNETT, CHARLES	2012	90kg
CRONIN, PATRICK	2013	81kg
DOMINIAK, ARTUR	2010	90kg
DONALDSON, SPENSER	2012	73kg
ELLIS, SAMUEL**	2012	66kg
EYRE, SEAN	2012	81kg
FANT, ANDREW**	2011	100+kg
GIBSON, MICHAEL	2012	100kg
HOCHERTZ, NICHOLAS**	2011	100kg
HORSWILL, NATHAN**	2010	66kg
JUNG, SANG-WON**	2012	66kg
KELSEY, SHAUN	2012	81kg
KILGROE, KRISTOPHER	2010	90kg
LIN, ARTHUR	2012	73kg
MCCURDY, DAVID	2010	90kg
MCCOY, JOSIAH	2011	60kg
PIERCE, CHRISTIAN	2010	63kg
RIVERA, PABLO	2012	63kg
ROAN, JAMES	2010	73kg
SANDHAUS, JOSHUA	2011	73kg
SCHLAUCH, KYLE**	2012	100+KG

NAME	CLASS	Div
SINGLEY, PATRICK**	2012	90kg
SONG, MATTHEW# **	2010	81kg
TOIGONBAEV, SAMAT	2013	73kg
VARANELLI-DICCICO, DANIEL #	2010	100kg
WAHLQUIST, NICHOLAS	2012	100kg
WILSON, RYAN	2013	66kg
TAUCHNITZ, NORMAN	INT	81kg
SAWADA, KOHEI	INT	60kg

Team Captains

** All-American

AY10 Women's Team

NAME	CLASS	DIV
BATCHELDER, STEPHANIE	2013	70kg
CLARKE-POUNDER, CATHERINE	2013	70kg
DONOHOE, KATHERINE	2013	52kg
ESPINOSA-LEVY, ARIEL	2010	52kg
KABIRI, NARGIS **	2010	78kg
MUNOZ, DANIELLE	2011	63kg
PURKEY, HEATHER**	2012	63kg
TUDOR, LARISA**	2013	70kg

Team Captains

**All-American

AY11 Men's Team

NAME	CLASS	Div
ADEZ, ANTHONY	2011	73kg
ADKINS, JUSTIN**	2013	100+kg
BARNES, JOHN**	2013	66kg
BENNETT, CHARLES	2012	90kg
BOWMAN, AUSTIN	2014	81kg
CHAVEZ, BROCK	2011	60kg
CRONIN, PATRICK	2013	81kg
DONALDSON, SPENSER	2012	73kg
ELLIS, SAMUEL	2012	66kg
EYRE, SEAN	2012	81kg
FANT, ANDREW	2011	100+kg
GIAMMARIA, CARSON	2014	63kg
GIBSON, MICHAEL	2012	100kg
HOCHERTZ, NICHOLAS # **	2011	100kg
JUNG, SANG-WON**	2012	66kg
KELSEY, SHAUN	2012	81kg
KELLY, PATRICK	2014	73kg
KIM, RICHARD	2014	60kg
LIN, ARTHUR	2012	73kg
MCCOY, JOSIAH	2011	60kg
MIRANDA, MIKE	2014	81kg
PATTEN, STEPHEN	2014	90kg
PURITZ, JOEL	2014	73kg
REED, CARSON	2013	100kg
RIVERA, PABLO	2012	63kg
SANDHAUS, JOSHUA**	2011	73kg
SANDS, SAMUEL	2014	60kg
SCHLAUCH, KYLE**	2012	100+kg

NAME	CLASS	Div
SINGLEY, PATRICK	2012	90kg
TOIGONBAEV, SAMAT	2013	73kg
WAHLQUIST, NICHOLAS	2012	100kg

\# Team Captains

**All-American

AY11 Women's Team

NAME	CLASS	Div
BORDENAVE, MEAGAN	2014	63kg
CLARKE-POUNDER, CATHERINE	2013	78kg
DONOHOE, KATHERINE	2013	57kg
HERNANDEZ, KRISTEN**	2014	78+kg
ESPINOSA-LEVY, ARIEL	2012	52kg
MUNOZ, DANIELLE \# **	2011	73kg
POSEY, ELIZABETH	2014	78kg
PURKEY, HEATHER	2012	81kg
TALAVERA, JULIET**	2014	52kg
TUDOR, LARISA**	2013	70kg
WEBBER, CANDACE	2014	70kg

\# Team Captains

** All-American

AY12 Men's Team

NAME	CLASS	Div
ADKINS, JUSTIN	2013	100+kg
BARNES, JOHN	2013	66kg
BENNETT, CHARLES	2012	90kg
BOWMAN, AUSTIN	2014	81kg
CLEGG, JOSEPH	2013	90kg
CRONIN, PATRICK	2013	81kg
DIEHL, PATRICK	2014	90kg
DONALDSON, SPENSER	2012	73kg
ELLIS, SAMUEL #	2012	66kg
GIAMMARIA, CARSON	2014	63kg
JACOBSON, AARON	2013	90kg
JUNG, SANG-WON **	2012	66kg
KELSEY, SHAUN	2012	81kg
KELLY, PATRICK	2014	73kg
KIM, RICHARD	2014	60kg
LIN, ARTHUR	2012	73kg
LONG, JAMES	2013	81kg
MCKENNA, JOE	2013	81kg
MENDOZA, RICHARD	2014	100+kg
MIRANDA, MIKE	2014	81kg
MOOKEJEE, DEBRAJ	2013	100kg
PATTEN, STEPHEN	2014	90kg
PENNELL, JOSHUA	2015	66kg
PURITZ, JOEL	2014	73kg
PURKEY, JACOB	2015	66kg
REED, CARSON	2013	100kg
RIVERA, PABLO	2012	63kg
SANDS, SAMUEL	2014	60kg

NAME	CLASS	Div
SINGLEY, PATRICK	2012	90kg
SHUBERT, GARRETT	2013	100+kg
SCIUVA, ANTHONY	2013	90kg
TALLEY, MICHAEL	2014	81kg

Team Captains

** All-American

AY12 Women's Team

NAME	CLASS	Div
CLARKE-POUNDER, CATHERINE	2013	78kg
DONOHOE, KATHERINE	2013	57kg
ESPINOSA-LEVY, ARIEL	2012	52kg
LEWIS, EMILY	2014	57kg
LOSS, KATIE	2014	52kg
OLIVER, RACHEL	2014	63kg
POSEY, ELIZABETH	2014	78kg
PURKEY, HEATHER #	2012	81kg
TALAVERA, JULIET	2014	52kg
TUDOR, LARISA	2013	70kg
WEBBER, CANDACE	2014	70kg

Team Captains

** All-American

AY13 Men's Team

NAME	CLASS	Div
ADKINS, JUSTIN **	2013	100+kg
BARNES, JOHN # **	2013	66kg
BOWMAN, AUSTIN	2014	81kg
CLEGG, JOSEPH	2013	90kg
CRONIN, PATRICK #	2013	81kg
DAY, MATTHEW	2016	81kg
DIEHL, PATRICK	2014	90kg
FISHER, DOMINIQUE	2016	73kg
GIAMMARIA, CARSON	2014	63kg
HOGAN, PATRICK	2016	81kg
JACOBSON, AARON	2013	90kg
KELLY, PATRICK	2014	73kg
KIM, RICHARD	2014	60kg
LIN, FRANK	2016	60kg
LONG, JAMES	2013	81kg
MANGUS, JAKE	2016	81kg
MCKENNA, JOE	2013	81kg
MENDOZA, RICHARD **	2014	100+kg
MIRANDA, MIKE	2014	81kg
MOOKEJEE, DEBRAJ	2013	100kg
NORMAN, JOHN	2016	100+kg
PATTEN, STEPHEN	2014	90kg
PENNELL, JOSHUA	2015	66kg
PURITZ, JOEL	2014	73kg
PURKEY, JACOB	2015	66kg
REED, CARSON	2013	100kg
SANDS, SAMUEL	2014	60kg
SHUBERT, GARRETT	2013	100+kg

NAME	CLASS	Div
STANLEY, PETER	2016	60kg
SCIUVA, ANTHONY	2013	90kg
TALLEY, MICHAEL	2014	81kg
UNDERWOOD, KYLE	2015	81KG

Team Captains

** All-American

AY13 Women's Team

NAME	CLASS	Div
CLARKE-POUNDER, CATHERINE	2013	78kg
CUOTTEAU, CHARLENE	2016	70kg
DIXON, SHERVON	2015	48kg
DONOHOE, KATHERINE	2013	57kg
GOODMAN, SARAH	2015	52kg
HANSEN, TIARA	2016	78kg
KAKOULAKIS, SODERIA	2016	57kg
LEWIS, EMILY	2014	57kg
LOSS, KATIE	2014	52kg
OLIVER, RACHEL	2014	63kg
PATTON, CARLY **	2016	63kg
POSEY, ELIZABETH	2014	78kg
TALAVERA, JULIET	2014	52kg
TUDOR, LARISA # **	2013	70kg
VARGAS, MELISSA	2014	70kg
WEBBER, CANDACE	2014	70kg

Team Captains

** All-American

AY14 Men's Team

NAME	CLASS	Div
BOWMAN, AUSTIN #	2014	81kg
DAY, MATTHEW	2016	81kg
DIEHL, PATRICK	2014	90kg
FISHER, DOMINIQUE	2016	73kg
GIAMMARIA, CARSON # **	2014	66kg
HALL, LAUREN	2017	66kg
HOGAN, PATRICK	2016	81kg
JACOBSON, AARON	2013	90kg
KELLY, PATRICK	2014	73kg
LIN, FRANK	2016	60kg
MANGUS, JAKE	2016	81kg
MIKINSKI, BRADLEY	2017	100kg
MIRANDA, MIKE	2014	81kg
MENDOZA, RICHARD **	2014	100+kg
MOON, SHINJOONG	2017	81kg
NORMAN, JOHN	2016	100+kg
PATTEN, STEPHEN	2014	90kg
PENNELL, JOSHUA	2015	66kg
PURITZ, JOEL	2014	73kg
PURKEY, JACOB	2015	66kg
ROTH, RYAN	2017	73kg
SANTOS, JOHN	2017	90kg
SNOW, CHASE	2015	66kg
STANLEY, PETER	2016	60kg
TALLEY, MICHAEL	2014	81kg
TSOEU, PAGIWA	2017	66kg
TING, NELSON	2017	81kg
UNDERWOOD, KYLE **	2015	73kg

AY14 Women's Team

NAME	CLASS	Div
BROOKS, PEARL	2017	57kg
CUOTTEAU, CHARLENE	2016	70kg
DIXON, SHERVON	2015	48kg
GERALD, CIARA	2017	78kg
GOODMAN, SARAH	2015	52kg
KAKOULAKIS, SODERIA	2016	57kg
HANSEN, TIARA	2016	78kg
LEWIS, EMILY	2014	57kg
LOSS, KATIE	2014	52kg
OLIVER, RACHEL	2014	63kg
PATTON, CARLY **	2016	63kg
POSEY, ELIZABETH **	2014	78kg
ROBERTS, SARA **	2015	70kg
TALAVERA, JULIET #	2014	52kg
VARGAS, MELISSA	2014	70kg
WEBBER, CANDACE	2014	70kg

Team Captains

** All-American

Appendix II - Recommendations from Cadets for LTC Morales' Coach K Award – Impacting Lives through Judo

The primary purpose behind sharing the letters and statements in these two appendixes is to allow the reader to see the impact of the program through the eyes of the cadet-athletes. Leaders plan and execute programs, but they will never know how effective these programs are until they gather data directly from the participants. In these statements, all given voluntarily, the athletes share their perspective of the program and how it influenced them as students and as athletes.

Cadet Pearl Brooks, Class 2016

I have never been on a team that felt so much like family before I joined the Army Judo Team. The man largely responsible for creating this culture on our team is LTC Hector Morales.

The first time I saw him was at Judo try-outs; to me at that point, he was just another man in the room who would be deciding whether by the end of the week I would have the privilege of calling myself a West Point Judo player. I learned later that he was, in fact, the head coach, and over the months of training from September to March in preparation for collegiate nationals, I gradually pieced together the story of our team and LTC Morales' remarkable role in it. I learned about the team's transition from being other teams' "warm-up" into a team that fiercely defends national titles every year. I have seen first-hand in practice every day how much it has been LTC Morales' clear vision, his driving commitment to the sport of Judo, and unrelenting faith in our ability and the potential for excellence that has taken the team on that incredible six-year journey. Even beyond his personal competency in the sport and his ability to motivate us and "make our butterflies [of nervousness] fly in formation" before competitions, LTC Morales pushes us to value character in competition. As he has said, when he is the referee for our matches at a tournament, it is harder for us to get a full point than when other teams' coaches ref us, so that there is not any doubt that West Point judokas earn their victories.

With his impending retirement, I do not think there is a single one of us on the team who will not miss Sensei Morales' humor on the mat and his constant, very vocal stream of advice, encouragement, and chastisement during practices. Most of all, though, I am grateful to him for making the team what it is today and giving us such an inspiring legacy to carry forward with us into the team's future. It is an honor now to become a part of the West Point Judo Team's story, and he is the reason why. LTC Morales has been more successful than any other coach I know in not only embodying the Army values and the values of a "sport-educator" that Coach Krzyzewski promotes but transmitting those values to his cadet-athletes and onto "the fields of friendly strife."

Cadet Austin Bowman, Class 2013

I am absolutely convinced that the success of the Judo Team over the last several years – winning national championships, placing cadets on the US national roster, and defeating international-level competitors – can be attributed in large part to the leadership of LTC Morales. He brings world-class technical skills and experience as well as organizational and leadership skills to carefully manage the training program of the team. Perhaps more importantly, LTC Morales has personally inspired me to become the best athlete that I can be. I see him as a huge role model, and he has been one of my closest mentors during my time here at the Academy. I think he is exceptionally deserving of the Coach K Award for this year.

Cadet Melissa Vargas, Class 2013

LTC Morales is an exceptional coach who effortlessly inspires his team and his students to live the Army Values through sport. Though he has a strong influence, he does not impose his opinions and instead guides and mentors Cadets. His work ethic, expertise, and above all his genuine love for us and Judo motivate and inspire us to be more than our best.

LTC Morales holds us to a high physical standard. He can tell when the team as a whole is drained and will only then make the call not to push us too far during practice. Other than that, he does not cut corners and knows that we do not expect him to let us do the same. Practice time is always at maximum effort. He respects how hard we work and never loses his temper with us in a way that would discourage our fighting strategies or make us lose faith in our abilities. Our relationship is precious to him; he is hard, but he's fair.

He knows that he does not have to coach us as extensively as he does. He selflessly pours hours of time and effort to make sure that we get to trip sections safe and coordinate events. He has personally called my TAC officer to negotiate terms on which I could attend nationals and contribute to my team. He is directly sought out other officers rather than relying on email leadership. Each Cadet is special to him and will work hard for us on the individual and team levels.

Yes, this sport demands a lot of time, and it's prioritized, but LTC Morales is an Army officer and makes sure that we know Judo applies to our careers in the Army. As a non-graduate, his love for us and West Point speaks volumes of his sense of duty. Part of his duty as an Army officer at West Point is to build us into warriors that can step into a situation where everything depends on our individual efforts, have the odds against us, and still return victorious. I was injured during the first semester, and he absolutely refused to let me do more than he thought I should. Not because I cannot handle it, but because he was not going to risk my health and future in the Army. He and the other coaches made it clear that the number one priority is not Judo, it is making sure that I commission as the leader the Army deserves.

Our coach may get fired up at matches and steam up at bad calls, but he is no sore loser, and he is never disrespectful no matter the situation. He is honorable, and his loyalty to the Army and the Army Judo Team would never lead him to project a negative image on our Academy. As the NCJA President, he has taken additional responsibilities that require his exceptional character.

Aside from being our fearless leader, we look up to him as a mentor. His family is as much a part of the team as he is. He makes his home open to all of us and entertains any concerns or questions we have about the Army, West Point, and life in general. In the Dojo, he gives us suggestions for techniques that we are practicing. He never tells us we are too short or too tall to pull off a throw in competition, but he will correct our form or modify it so that we are a more effective and deadly force. Another focus of his is ensuring that we are confident and in great mental health before a competition. Some practices end with muscle group and performance visualization drills. He guides us physically and mentally.

Overall, LTC Morales inspires and motivates us just by his presence. I do not push myself just when he is nearby. On an occasional day, he misses practice; I will repeat the team goals in my head and push myself that much harder. Then I look around and see my teammates also working to muscle failure and everyone in the room are cheering each other on, saying things like, "Let's go! Good Job, you will need it at nationals! They will not know what hit 'em!" Our competition never gets used to us. People who've been doing Judo since childhood get beaten out by Cadets who have four years or less of experience.

Recruited teams do not appreciate that we regularly take three 1st place trophies out of four divisions.

I have seen Cadets start Judo in all forms: arrogant, lazy, timid, doubtful, you name it. The greatest achievement is how this man's character and spirit affects the team in a kind of groupthink like we've never experienced before and by the end of the year, we are noticeably better than we were before, both physically and mentally. We remain united towards our common goals from the beginning of the semester, hold each other to high standards even after nationals, always motivate each other, and we mentor each other even at the Cadet level. LTC Morales does not just build or breed warriors just to fight on the mat; he builds the officers that we need. Watching my peers grow like that is a little scary, but mostly it is an exciting and beautiful thing to see.

CDT Frank Lin, Class 2016

LTC Morales has always been the core of the team since day one. He has given his complete dedication in making sure that we not only succeed as a team, but we bond and build the strongest and tightest relationship as fellow warriors. He has made countless sacrifices by always showing up to practices, both morning and afternoon, and is always with us on our competitions to lead us to victory.

He has inspired the beginners and newcomers of this team to work hard and never to give up. Starting from the very first day, he gave all the new members of the team a goal, a goal to become the best Judo team in collegiate Judo and to win the Collegiate National title. LTC Morales taught us never to look away from the goal and always to stay motivated, no matter how repetitive and challenging practice gets.

For the veterans and the advanced members of the team, he has also inspired them a lot. Instead of simply showing them what to do, he has taught them how to teach the new members of the team and how to become leaders. That is what is truly special about LTC Morales. He will show you how to be a great athlete and more importantly, he will show you how to train the rest of your peers to become great as well.

Many people see Judo as an individual sport where the competition is one-on-one. Being on this team and after being coached by LTC Morales, I no longer see Judo as an individual sport. Judo is just as much as a team sport as football or basketball. He taught us in Judo, you train with your teammates, those teammates are the ones who make you a better judoka, and the ones who help you succeed. He has shown us that our teammates are the ones who push us hardest when we spar, always giving us feedback on the mistakes, we make, and on things we can improve. Most importantly, he has taught us that we are not only fighting for ourselves and the sport of Judo but for our team, the Army team as a whole.

CDT Juliet Talavera, Class 2013

LTC Morales has been my coach for the last four years. If I can be half of the leader that he is, I would consider myself successful. LTC Morales leads by example and, at the end of the day; I never doubted that he cares about the team. Even though he has other priorities, LTC Morales has stated many times that practice and being around us is the best part of his day. Personally, even after having a terrible day, Judo practice is the 2 hours where nothing else matters. Like LTC Morales, Judo practice is my favorite time of day. It would not be true of LTC Morales did not foster such a positive work environment.

As a coach, LTC Morales inspires everyone on the team to excel. He understands that everyone is different and, uses different means to motivate us. That just shows how much he cares about our development as athletes. Moreover, LTC Morales was my mentor during PL300 and shed valuable insight during our meetings. Not only was he a phenomenal coach, but he was also an outstanding leader. He shared his leadership philosophy with me, which, in turn, made me evaluate my philosophy. I would be lying if I did not confess that I took a few of his tenets and incorporated them into mine. Not only does he care about our athletic development, but LTC Morales also seeks to develop us all as leaders. He constantly reminds all of us of the team about how Judo translates into being a leader in the Army. LTC Morales serves as an inspiration to everyone on the team. We will be sad to see him go when he retires in May, but he has left a lasting, positive impact on the team.

LTC Morales' 2014 Coach K Award Ceremony

(Photo Courtesy of BySoledad Photography)

Appendix III – A Tribute to Sensei Reno – 2010 Nomination for the Coach K Award

As stated throughout this book, feats of great performance cannot be done in a vacuum and you most align with people who believe the same you believe and are willing to work with you side by side through the challenges and adversities. Sensei Reno was the one I relied on to keep the mat in check when I was at extended meetings and could not make it to the mat. He also gave technical foundation and fighting guidance to all the athletes. He was all in and committed to the plan more than anyone else. As he would always say, *"Papi, I have your back! Whatever we need to do, it will be done."* In 2010, I submitted Sensei Reno for the Coach K Award. He earned this recognition every day but hopefully he knows that the respect we have for him is the best award you can ever get. Below is the nomination we submitted on his behalf.

Sensei Emilio "Reno" Claudio is an icon with the West Point Judo program and has made contributions to the physical development of the leaders of our Army for the last 20 years. His contributions also extend to the community and he was the head instructor of the West Point kids' program for many years. While working with kids in Judo and jujitsu during the late 80s and early 90s, cadets from the Judo team came around and participated in these classes to improve their technique. In 1998, due to his knowledge, professionalism, and the respect cadets and I had for his passion, I added him formally as a coach for the West Point Judo team. He has been the constant face of this program for over a decade. Many of the cadets he mentored achieved their black belts through the Hoteikan System. He has helped develop athletes from white belts to Collegiate National Champions. His dedication to the sport of Judo and to the development of these young leaders is unparalleled.

Sensei Reno has contributed to building leaders of character in the Judo program for more than a decade. Since 1998, he has volunteered his time and efforts to build leaders and to promote the tenants of the art of Judo, mutual welfare and benefit and maximum efficiency, along with duty, honor, and country among these young officers. Because he has been the constant face of this Judo program since the late nineties, Sensei Reno has earned the trust and confidence of the members of the team, past and present. Many of the officers have stayed in touch with him and have even invited him to their weddings, family events, and some of them constantly celebrate successes and share their challenges with him.

Sensei Reno is from a completely different generation of martial artists where hard work, dedication, and perseverance were requirements for success in the arts without many of the aspects of psychology and science that we have today. However, we have seen him successfully adjust to inculcate these values to these new generations in very positive ways and with a caring approach that the cadet-athletes appreciate. Sensei Reno displays an extremely ethical and straightforward way of life and is a physical role model to all the young members of the Judo team. At age 72, Sensei Reno never misses practice or trip sections and is always ready to jump in to train when someone needs a partner...he is an inspiration to all the officers and cadets that encounter him.

In addition to coaching the Judo program, he stays after practice to work with individual cadets in the Hoteikan Jujitsu Self-Defense program. On this program, he is the head sensei Nationwide for the Hoteikan System and has promoted more than ten cadets to black belt under that system.

Sensei Reno lives the values we attempt to inculcate to our athletes. He is the ultimate volunteer and has represented the Academy and the West Point Judo team at the Air Force Academy, RMC, and multiple national level events. He has earned the respect of the cadet-athletes, officer representatives, DPE faculty, and the community at large. Recognizing him with this award will elevate the standards for coaches and volunteers in the future. While he already has the respect and admiration of everyone on this program, in his words "the greatest reward", recognizing him with this well-deserved award will reinforce that his over decade-long efforts are noted and appreciated.

Sensei Reno's 2010 Coach K Award Ceremony

(Photo Courtesy of BySoledad Photography)

About the Author

Dr. Morales started his military career as a non-English speaking Infantry Soldier in Fort Benning, Georgia. He attended the University of Puerto Rico where he was a Judo and Wrestling athlete, completed a degree in physical education, and received a commission as an officer in the U.S. Army in 1990. He was a member of the Armed Forces Judo Team and led the program from 2003 until 2013. He is an Army Master Fitness Trainer and Army Master Combatives Instructor. In 1998, he received a Master's Degree in Kinesiology from the University of Georgia and became an instructor of physical education at the U.S. Military Academy at West Point. During his first tour at West Point, he instructed cadets in personal fitness, wellness, unit fitness program development, Judo, and self-defense, and he was the head coach for the West Point Judo Team. After leaving the Academy, he was responsible for sports and fitness programs

for Army Soldiers in South Korea, trained Soldiers in Fort Bliss, Texas to lead the new Army Physical Readiness program, and established the Army Combatives Program at Fort Bliss. Over his career, Dr. Morales certified over 1,500 Soldiers and cadets as Army combatives instructors.

In 2004, Dr. Morales was selected to become an Academy Professor of Physical Education at West Point and became the first Hispanic ever selected for this position. In 2005, he attended Florida State University to complete his doctorate in sport and exercise psychology and reported to the academy in 2008. As an Academy Professor, Dr. Morales was Deputy Director, Director of Program Support, Director of Competitive Clubs, coached the West Point Judo Team, Course Director for personal fitness, combatives instructor certification, basic Judo instruction, and nutrition for performance.

In 2010, Dr. Morales became a Certified Performance Enhancement Consultant through the Association for Applied Sports Psychology (AASP), and he has worked with athletes at the developmental, collegiate, and professional levels.

In 2010, Dr. Morales led the West Judo Team to their first national title in 50 years, and in 2011 the team won all the team divisions of the NCJA National Championships, becoming the first and only team to complete that feat in the history of the National Collegiate Judo Association.

Dr. Morales retired from the Army as a Lieutenant Colonel in 2014 and joined the Pittsburgh Pirates' Mental Conditioning Team.